THE "I Will" PROMISES OF CHRIST

Promises giving assurance in times of uncertainty

The "I Will" PROMISES of CHRIST

Promises giving assurance in times of uncertainty

IAN FLECK

AMBASSADOR INTERNATIONAL
GREENVILLE, SOUTH CAROLINA & BELFAST, NORTHERN IRELAND

www.ambassador-international.com

The "I Will" Promises of Christ
Promises giving assurance in times of uncertainty

Paperback: ISBN: 978-1-62020-982-0
eBook: ISBN: 978-1-62020-996-7

Printed in UK

Ambassador International
Emerald House
411 University Ridge, Suite B14
Greenville, SC 29601
www.ambassador-international.com

Ambassador Books and Media
The Mount
2 Woodstock Link
Belfast, BT6 8DD, Northern Ireland, UK
www.ambassadormedia.co.uk

This book is dedicated to our grandchildren

Praying that they will experience the blessing
of these promises of Christ upon their lives.

Contents

Any book that points us to Christ is always worth reading. By introducing us to our Lord's "I will's" Ian's book certainly does that. He has dealt with them in a clear and practical way and his explanation of certain biblical words has been most enlightening and very helpful in adding further clarity to the message. Those who read this book will be both challenged and encouraged by these statements of our Lord.

Rev. Tom Shaw
Past President of the Faith Mission

Ian Fleck has written a biblically rich and practically helpful book that takes us through the "I will's" of Christ. Your mind will be stretched and your heart warmed at the range and depths of these studies. So much of who we are and what we have as believers rests on the explicit promises of our Saviour. These are the sure foundations of our soul.

Dr. Liam Goligher
Senior Minister of Tenth Presbyterian Church, Philadelphia

In a world of uncertainty where nothing can be taken at face value, this book reminds us of the unchanging nature of a dependable God who is faithful in both word and deed. It is an informative, enjoyable and uplifting read that brings comfort and assurance amidst the doubts and challenges of life.

Ronnie Armour
President Belfast City Mission

In this very good book Ian unpacks in a helpful way some of the life changing promises of Jesus Christ. He makes it abundantly clear that when Christ makes a promise He keeps it! When Christ says "I will" He means it! What a contrast to the fake news and empty promises which are such alarming marks of our contemporary culture. This book is about rock solid Christian basics which are a sure foundation for a Christ centred life. It is about promises which will be kept. It is about the Lord Jesus Christ who can be totally trusted. His promises hold true for this life... and the next! This book will both inform the mind and feed the soul. I warmly commend it.

Bishop Ken (Fanta) Clarke
Former Bishop of Kilmore, Elphin and Ardagh

Foreword

Ian Fleck has followed up his book on "The Twelve Chosen Disciples" with this study which focuses on the "I Will" promises of Christ. His purpose is to explore these words of Jesus as they are recorded in the Gospels. Nine of these have been selected and we are given a detailed exposition of each of these promises from the Master. Not only are they set in their immediate context but also in the context of the whole of Scripture.

Throughout there is a careful pastoral application which brings challenges and encouragement as well as reassurance and hope to the reader. This is not a book to be read straight through at one sitting, but the reader is prompted to take time to reflect upon each promise. Therefore the provision of a series of questions at the end of each section is a helpful addition for those who wish to consider the issues on a more personal level.

In presenting these studies, there is evidence of Ian's many years of Christian experience in Africa and Ireland. Consequently, he is to be commended for emphasising these wonderful promises of Jesus, which He declared with integrity and fulfilled with power.

This work is published in the prayerful hope that those who read it will take Jesus at His word, realising that He never makes an empty promise and is to be trusted completely, for all He promises is intended for our good and His glory.

Rev. Dr. John W. Lockington

Preface

In a court case the witness is normally asked, *"Do you promise* (solemnly swear) *to tell the truth, the whole truth and nothing but the truth?"* At a marriage ceremony the bridegroom is traditionally asked, *"Will you take...(bride) to be your wife? Will you promise to love her, comfort her, honour and protect her, and forsaking all others be faithful to her, as long as you both shall live?"* These are serious and solemn promises; however, it is regrettable that on many occasions they are not kept. Occasionally it has been proved in a court case that the witness did not tell the truth; also in society many marriages are broken because the promises made were not kept.

If you are sceptical of the promises Jesus made then I trust you will change your mind after reading this book. We will look at the special and unique character of Jesus who has made these wonderful promises, and the reason why we can trust and believe them. These promises can make a profound impact upon our lives and gives us the assurance that Jesus is with us in the times of stress and trouble. Jesus promised to give us rest and never to leave us nor forsake us.

God's promises challenge and remind us that He is trustworthy. Therefore it is good to read the promises about who God is and hold on to them that He is with us in our individual situations.

God gave Noah a rainbow as a sign that He would keep His promise and as He was faithful to Noah, He will be faithful to us. God promises to give us everything we need in our daily lives.

During His time on earth, Jesus made many promises about the peace and hope He offers us. Jesus' promises give us assurance that He truly is the Saviour of the world.

The most precious of all God's promises to us is the assurance of forgiveness and eternal life through the sacrifice of Christ on the cross. After His death and resurrection for our salvation, Jesus ascended back to heaven. He promised He would return so let us then be ready and waiting for that glorious day.

How does one express an adequate word of appreciation to those who were so kind in their support and assistance in bringing this book to its present state, without whom this study on the "I will" promises of Christ could not have been completed.

As the manuscript was being prepared I shared it with a number of friends. First of all, I am grateful to my wife Sandra, who has always been fully supportive of all my work and has spent many hours reading and re-reading the manuscript. My thanks also to Mr John Todd, Rev. Brian Smyth and the Rev. John Lockington, for the invaluable advice and help they gave. Without their help this book would not be as it is; I accept personal responsibility for any remaining weaknesses.

I express my sincere thanks and appreciation to Mr Ronnie Armour, Bishop Ken (Fanta) Clarke, Rev. Dr. Liam Goligher, Rev. Mark Meynell and Rev. Tom Shaw, for their kind comments of recommendation. I also thank the Rev. Dr. John Lockington for writing the Foreword.

This book is a modest attempt to summarise not only what the "I will" promises of Christ were, but what they mean. I trust you will be challenged and blessed as you read it.

Ian Fleck
February 2021

Introduction

We are all accustomed to promises that have been made and broken. There are many reasons why this happens. Sometimes we forget, or are negligent, and sometimes it may be due to circumstances beyond our control.

People may intend to do what they have promised but because of some unfortunate or unforeseen circumstance, they may not be able to do so. As human beings we are limited and can be prevented from carrying out our planned activities or commitment.

What about the promises of God? How certain are they? A promise is of no more value than the willingness and ability of the one who makes the promise to carry it through.

There are many "I will" promises that Christ made to the disciples and therefore, to all who will believe on His name. These special "I wills" give a solid foundation for our Christian faith as they provide comfort, consolation, strength and hope.

When we receive an invitation to a special function the first thing we do is to see who is giving the invitation. If we know the person well we will make a special effort to attend and that fundamental answer has an important bearing on the result.

As we read the Scriptures we see that Jesus on many occasions gives an invitation to follow Him, and before we accept those invitations and believe those promises, we need to know what authority or right He has for doing so.

There are a number of remarkable and outstanding things we can say about Jesus Christ.

The remarkable and unique birth of Jesus Christ

He is the subject of more than 300 Old Testament prophecies. His birth and the events of His life had been foretold by many prophets during a period of 1,500 years. History confirms that even the smallest detail happened just as predicted. It confirms beyond any doubt that Jesus is the true Messiah, the Son of God and Saviour of the world.

<u>Prophesied</u>	<u>Fulfilled in</u>
His Birth by Isaiah (Isaiah 7:14)	Matthew 1:18, 22-23
His Birthplace by Micah (Micah 5:2)	Luke 2: 4-7
His Childhood in Egypt by Hosea (Hosea 11:1)	Matthew 2:14-15
The Purpose of His Death by Isaiah (Isaiah 53:4-6)	1 Peter 2:24
His Betrayal by Zechariah (Zechariah 11:12-13)	Matthew 26:14-16; 27:3-10
His Crucifixion (Psalm 22)	Matthew 27
His Resurrection (Psalm 16:9-10)	Acts 2:31

The Bible tells us that Jesus existed as God from eternity past. There was never a "time" when He was not; Jesus Himself taught His eternal existence and claimed to have existed in heaven even before the creation of the universe (John 6:62, 8:58, 17:5, 24). Jesus said to the Pharisees who were arguing with Him how old He was, *"Truly, truly, I say to you, before Abraham was, I am"* (John 8:58).

The Bible makes it clear that Jesus, the second person of the Godhead, was involved in the creation of the entire universe and everything in heaven (including the angels) as described in Genesis 1 and 2. (John 1:3, Colossians 1:16-17, Hebrews 1:2).

The remarkable and outstanding life of Jesus Christ

God became man in Christ Jesus and took the form of a human being. He was a real, genuine, though sinless human. He *"made himself nothing, taking the form of a servant, being born in the likeness of men"* (Philippians 2:5-7) and was born as a baby in a stable in Bethlehem of Judea. The only person without sin ever born of woman was Christ.

He grew up as a man, teaching throughout Palestine and performing numerous miracles to validate His claims. Jesus constantly demonstrated power over sickness and disease. He made the lame to walk, the dumb to speak and the blind to see.

When a paralyzed man was let down through the roof of a house wanting to be healed by Him, Jesus said, *"Son, your sins are forgiven you."* The religious leaders immediately reacted. *"Why does this fellow talk like that? He's blaspheming! Who can forgive sins but God alone?"*

When Jesus was on trial for his life, the high priest put the question to him directly: *"Are you the Christ, the Son of the Blessed?"* Jesus said, *"I am, and you will see the Son of Man seated at the right hand of Power, and coming on the clouds of heaven."* The high priest tore his clothes and said, *"What further witnesses do we need? You have heard his blasphemy"* (Mark 14:61-63).

The beggar who sat outside the temple was well known. Jesus healed him and then the authorities questioned the beggar about what happened. He said, *"One thing I do know, that though I was blind, now I see!"* He was astounded that these religious authorities did not recognize this Healer as the Son of God. *"Never since the world began has it been heard that anyone opened the eyes of a man born blind. If this man were not from God, he could do nothing"* (John 9:25, 32). To the blind man the evidence that Jesus was a unique person was obvious.

Jesus also demonstrated a supernatural power over nature. With a statement only He stilled a raging storm of high wind and waves on the Sea of Galilee. Those in the boat were amazed, asking, *"Who is this? Even the wind and waves obey him!"* (Mark 4:39-41). He turned water into wine at a wedding (John 2:1-11). He fed a massive crowd of 5,000 people, starting with five loaves of bread and two fish (Matthew 14:13-21). He gave a grieving widow back her only son by raising him from the dead (Luke 7:11-17).

Lazarus, a friend of Jesus, died and was buried in a tomb for four days. When Jesus arrived at the tomb He said, *"Lazarus, come forth!"* (John 11:43) and he was raised from the dead. It is significant that His enemies did not deny this miracle. Rather, they decided to kill Him. They said *"If we let him go on like this, everyone will believe in him"* (John 11:48).

The remarkable and outstanding death of Jesus Christ

No event in history compares with the significance of the death of Christ. Many important things have happened in the world, but none can be compared with Christ's death.

Jesus' death was by public execution on a cross, a common form of torture and death, used by the Roman government. The accusation against Jesus was for blasphemy (for claiming to be God). Jesus was cruelly scourged and a mock crown of long thorns beaten into His head. They forced Him to walk to an execution hill outside of Jerusalem and crucified Him on a wooden cross.

After wine vinegar was put on a sponge and held up to Jesus, He said, *"It is finished"* and He bowed His head and gave up His spirit (John 19:20).

Five miraculous things were reported to have happened when Jesus died on the cross.

a) *"There was darkness over all the land"* (Matthew 27:45). On Friday from noon until 3pm the sky was dark. It is hard to imagine what the people were feeling when they saw this happening.

b) "*The curtain of the temple was torn in two, from top to bottom*" at the very moment when Jesus breathed His last breath (Matthew 27:51). This veil was actually between 30 and 60 feet high. Josephus reported that the veil was as thick as a man's hand (about 4 inches in thickness) and that horses tied to each other could not pull it apart, which would make it impossible for men to tear apart. It should be noted that it was torn from top to bottom showing that man was not responsible for the tearing of the curtain.

c) "*The earth shook, and the rocks split*" (Matthew 27:51). There was an earthquake that shook Calvary the moment Christ died. It was an extremely large endorsement of what Christ had done. It pointed to the magnitude of the death of Jesus Christ. The sudden shaking of the earth was at the exact moment that Jesus shouted the victory cry, "Finished" and gave His spirit back to the Father.

d) "*The tombs also were opened. And many bodies of the saints who had fallen asleep were raised*" (Matthew 27:52-53). Graves opened up and the saints came out and appeared to many people. It is very difficult to imagine what that looked like; the dead rising when Jesus died. This was a remarkable sequence of events.

e) "*When the centurion and those who were with him, keeping watch over Jesus, saw the earthquake and what took place, they were filled with awe and said, 'Truly this was the Son of God'*" (Matthew 27:54). Lives were changed and many people began to realise who Jesus was.

All of these amazing things can be said about the death of Jesus Christ.

The remarkable and extraordinary resurrection of Jesus Christ

The body of Jesus was taken from the cross by Joseph of Arimathea and wrapped in clean linen cloths. Joseph placed His body in his own new tomb, which he had cut out of the rock, and rolled a big stone in front of the entrance.

It was known that Jesus said He would rise from the dead in three days. So they stationed a guard of trained Roman soldiers at the tomb. A Roman official made the entrance secure by sealing the tomb to prevent anyone from secretly moving the stone.

In spite of all this, three days later the large stone was found to be moved from the entrance to the tomb. The body was gone. Only the linen cloths that had been around Jesus' body were found in the tomb. From the scriptural references we note that both the critics and the followers of Jesus are in agreement that the tomb was empty and the body missing.

Jesus' supreme evidence of deity was His own resurrection from the dead. Five times in the course of His life, Jesus clearly predicted that He would be killed and rise from the dead three days later. So by His own words, He offers this proof, *"The Son of Man must be delivered into the hands of sinful men and be crucified and on the third day rise"* (Luke 24:7).

Because Christ rose from the tomb on the third day we know that God exists. If Christ did not rise from the dead, Christianity has no authority or reality; also, the martyrs who went to the lions' den and missionaries who were killed while taking this message to others, have been deceived and achieved nothing.

Paul, the great apostle, wrote, *"If Christ has not been raised, then our preaching is in vain and your faith is in vain"* (1 Corinthians 15:14). Paul rested his argument on the bodily resurrection of Christ.

The earliest explanation circulated was that the disciples stole the body while the guards were sleeping. The chief priests gave the soldiers a large sum of money and said, *"Tell people, 'His disciples came by night and stole him away while we were asleep'"* (Matthew 28:13). It does not make sense to claim that an entire guard of highly trained Roman soldiers had fallen asleep while on duty, which was punishable by death.

On the other hand, if any of the officials had moved His body, or knew where it was, surely they would have presented it to prove Jesus had not risen from the dead. All four of the Gospel writers give accounts of Jesus showing up physically after his burial. On one occasion when Jesus appeared to His disciples, Thomas was not there. When they told Thomas that they had seen Jesus he would not believe them saying, *"Unless I see in his hands the mark of the nails, and place my finger into the mark of the nails, and place my hand into his side, I will never believe"* (John 20:25).

One week later when Jesus came to them again, Thomas was present. Jesus said to Thomas, *"Put your finger here, and see my hands; and put out your hand and place it in my side. Do not disbelieve, but believe."* Thomas replied, *"My Lord and my God!"* Jesus said to him, *"Have you believed because you have seen me? Blessed are those who have not seen and yet have believed"* (John 20:27-29).

Paul tells us that Jesus appeared to Peter and then to the Twelve, *"Then he appeared to more than five hundred brothers at one time"* (1 Corinthians 15:6). All these things are proof that Jesus Christ was an outstanding person who experienced an extraordinary and unique resurrection.

Jesus Christ made the promise "I will"

We have seen what is so special about Jesus Christ who made many "I will" promises. They are the promises of an extraordinary and unique person, Jesus Christ, the Son of God.

On one occasion Jesus asked His disciples, *"Who do people say the Son of Man is?"* They replied, *"Some say John the Baptist, others say Elijah, and others Jeremiah or one of the prophets."* Then Jesus said to them, *"But who do you say that I am?"* Then Simon Peter answered, *"You are the Christ, the Son of the living God"* (Matthew 16:13-16).

It is amazing to know that we have received some remarkable promises from Christ the promised Messiah to encourage us in our daily lives. This is what makes the promises so special.

Let us now study and consider the 'I will' promises of Jesus that can influence our lives.

1

The "I Will" of Rest

Jesus said, *"Come to me, all who labour and are heavy laden, and I WILL give you rest."*
(Matthew 11:28)

The word "rest" is one of those words that can be expressed in a variety of ways. "Rest" is defined as "to relax, take a break, be at peace, be at ease or have a time of refreshment." The Bible often speaks of rest, beginning with the week when God created all things. We are told how the work of creation was completed in six days and then, *"he rested on the seventh day from all his work that he had done* (Genesis 2:2). God rested, not because He was tired but simply stopped what He was doing, to set the example for mankind to follow. The fourth of the Ten Commandments made resting on the Sabbath a requirement of the Law (Exodus 20:8-11).

The command to rest was not an excuse to be lazy. Man and beast were to work for six days and then rest on the Sabbath day. The land also needed to rest (Leviticus 25:4, 8-12). Many people feel they must be constantly working seven days a week to achieve all they want to do. However, God instructs us to rest because of the advantages it gives.

For the Christian, the greatest and most meaningful rest is found in Christ. He invites "all who *labour and are heavy laden,*" to come to Him (Matthew 11:28) and cast their cares on Him (1 Peter 5:7). It is only in Him that we find absolute rest.

p 28

The Jews were constantly struggling and labouring in an effort to make their lives acceptable to God. They were trying to obey many restrictions imposed upon them by obeying their ceremonial laws, but it is Christ alone who makes atonement for sin. *"For our sake he made him to be sin who knew no sin, so that in him we might become the righteousness of God"* (2 Corinthians 5:21).

Who are those who Labour and are Heavy Laden?

Many people are seeking rest from the trials and burdens of life, but cannot find it in wealth or in pleasure. They would give their well earned money for this rest if it was for sale, but it cannot be bought in a shop or market place. The rest that Jesus has promised is very comforting to people in many situations.

Those seeking to keep religious laws

To appreciate our Lord's invitation, we must recognise that the Lord was addressing the people of Israel who were burdened and weighed down with the effort of seeking to keep the Mosaic Law and the legal laws of the Pharisees. Neither Moses nor the Pharisees could give rest from the pressing burden or offer release from the heavy load that the Law brought.

"The Law was given through Moses" (John 1:17), and because the Pharisees considered themselves the Law's official interpreters, they elevated themselves to a position of authority in Israel. In Matthew 23:2 we read, *"The scribes and the Pharisees sit on Moses' seat, so practise and observe whatever they tell you, but not what they do. For they preach, but do not practise."*

Christ referred to the scribes and the Pharisees as men who "sit on Moses' seat." As interpreters and teachers of the Law, the Pharisees claimed the authority of Moses. They also demanded that all Israelites who submitted to Moses, should also submit to them.

The Lord warned the people of the repressive and legalistic ways of the Pharisees. He said, *"Woe to you lawyers also! For you load people with burdens hard to bear, and you yourselves do not touch the burdens with one of your fingers"* (Luke 11:46).

Jesus was not referring to the difficulty and tiredness of physical labour, but to spiritual weariness. This came to those exhausted from following all the religious rules and keeping up all the religious appearances that were required of the Jews. The result would be the dissatisfaction, guilt and frustration that always go with legalism (a system of rules and regulations for achieving both salvation and spiritual growth. Legalists believe in, and demand, a strict literal adherence to rules and regulations). To them the obedience to the Law, not faith in God's grace, was the sole principle of redemption.

The Lord Jesus had more hostility from the legalists of His day than any other group. It was not the thief or the immoral person who put Jesus on the cross - it was the legalists. Jesus pronounced six woes on the Pharisees in which He gave some of the specific problems with legalism (Luke 11:37-54). Jesus was speaking about the way the Pharisees had hidden the true meaning of the Old Testament Law with their own religious rules and regulations, placing excessive emphasis on outward appearance, also following a set of strict laws and instructions, as the way to God and as a way to receive God's blessing in life.

At the root of legalism is the sin of pride, because the legalist thinks that he is able to commend himself to God by his own good deeds. Religion without God is always trying to make the person look good, but it neglects the fact that the Lord looks on the heart.

The Talmud (a collection of writings that covers the full range of Jewish law and tradition), states that they had classified the Mosaic Law into 613 Commandments - 248 Positive Commandments (do's) and 365 Negative Commandments (don'ts).

Even though the Old Testament Law was good, holy and righteous, it was weak and did not bring liberty because of its dependence on human effort. It left people feeling guilty because of their failure to remove their sin. Rather than freedom, it brought bondage and instead of a sense of release, it brought a sense of guilt and failure.

Jesus understood the burden of the Jewish faith to follow the Law and was inviting those under this stress and strain to come to Him for His yoke was easy and His burden was light (Matthew 11:30).

Those seeking to obey man-made laws

A conscientious, law-abiding Jew was expected to keep several hundred man-made laws. When Jesus healed someone on the Sabbath day the Pharisees raised strong objections about the breaking of their rules. They prohibited the giving of aid to anyone who was ill on the Sabbath unless that person's life was in danger (Luke 6:11). They proclaimed that a Jew could only travel 1,000 yards from their home on the Sabbath and allowed the tying of a knot only if it could be untied with one hand.

They also stated that the plucking the ears of corn on the Sabbath and rubbing them in their hands before eating the grain, amounted to reaping and threshing (Luke 6:1-2). When a Pharisee invited Jesus to dinner, He did not get involved in their elaborate washing custom and when they questioned Him about it, He criticised them for their hypocrisy (Luke 11:38-41).

The Pharisees saw themselves as good people because they kept the Law and not as sinners in need of a Saviour. However, Jesus said they ought to be as careful about clean hearts as they were about clean hands.

Jesus condemned the Pharisees because they loved to be in the front seats in the synagogues and to receive the respectful greetings in the market places. They wanted people to notice how important they were (Luke 11:43).

Jesus came to free His people from the intolerable traditions of the Jewish elders, to cancel those unscriptural regulations, and introduce a purer and more spiritual way of worship. Therefore this invitation was extended to those who were weary and oppressed by the heavy load of rules and regulations placed upon them by the scribes and Pharisees (Matthew 23:4).

Those seeking salvation by their own efforts

Christ's invitation to come to Him is as relevant today as it was at the time when Jesus walked on earth. It applies to those who, for whatever reason, try to achieve salvation by means of their own efforts.

Christ addresses *"all who labour and are heavy laden"* - it is a wide description. It includes multitudes in this weary world - all are invited, whoever they may be, and whatever their past lives - to come to Christ.

It is in the midst of this religious setting that the Lord makes a very gracious invitation to all who would want to experience the relief, joy and the blessing of His life through a grace/faith relationship with Him.

Jesus always invites desperate, helpless and seemingly hopeless people to come to Him. *"When he saw the crowds, he had compassion for them, because they were harassed and helpless, like sheep without a shepherd"* (Matthew 9:36).

Martin Luther entered a monastery to separate himself from the world. He endured great humiliation in the search of holiness and peace. If ever a monk could obtain heaven by his works, it was Luther, for he had been encouraged to satisfy God's justice by his many good works. He tortured himself almost to the point of death to obtain peace with God for his troubled heart, but was unsuccessful.

Many people are like Luther, hoping and believing that their good living and their good works will be enough to get them to heaven. It was only when Luther came to realise his good works could contribute nothing towards his salvation, that he found his sins forgiven and peace with God.

Those who seek to earn credit towards their salvation are frequently searching for rest of soul and peace with God. But Jesus says, *"I will give you rest."* The dictionary describes 'rest' as cessation from action, motion, labour, or exertion. To enter God's rest is to cease from all efforts at self-help in trying to earn salvation.

Those who are weary and burdened, by making every effort to gain salvation, must take it as a gift from Jesus who came from heaven. *"For by grace you have been saved through faith... it is the gift of God, not a result of works, so that no one may boast"* (Ephesians 2:8-9).

What is their Rest?

"Rest" is something everyone needs from time to time. We long for it and work to achieve it but very often it evades us, but Jesus said to his disciples, *"Come away by yourselves to a desolate place and rest a while"* (Mark 6:31). The Lord knew the value of rest. However, on this occasion, Jesus meant more than rest from toil and labour or from a weary journey.

What is the nature of this "rest" which Christ gives to all who come to Him? It is a spiritual rest, a satisfying rest, a "rest for the soul" as the Saviour declares later in this passage. It is a rest that this world cannot give.

It is good to understand that because of where the invitation comes from, the promise will be fulfilled. He said, *"I will give."* Therefore, as a result of who He is, there can be no doubt; He has the power and ability to do what He says.

Now, what is promised? He promises *"I will give you rest"* and this rest is far reaching. We are so busy with the affairs of everyday living that we find ourselves struggling with life rather than enjoying it. We are living in the most restless age that has ever been known in this world. Men and women are restless - they have no peace of mind, heart or conscience. But Jesus promises rest to *"all"* who come to Him.

He gives rest of heart

One of the most dreaded diseases in the world today is what we call "heart trouble" and often we hear of someone afflicted by a heart attack. The heart beats an average of 75 beats a minute, 40 million times a year. But one day when we least expect it, our heart will beat for the last time and when it does, life as we know it, will be over for us.

One of the most painful emotional experiences is that of a "broken heart" whether it is from the illness or death of a loved one, or for some other personal problem. In John 14, Jesus is not talking about physical heart trouble but about a spiritual illness. He is talking about a troubled, burdened or sorrowful heart.

Therefore, comforting words are found in John 14:1, *"Let not your hearts be troubled. Believe in God; believe also in me."* The broken, lonely or sad heart will find rest in Jesus. When Jesus said these words His disciples did not understand that He was going to the cross to die for the sins of the world. All they knew was that Jesus was going to leave them and as a result they were filled with fear. It looked like their world was falling apart and darkness was about to overtake them, yet they were not to let their hearts be troubled.

Jesus gave three reasons why they should not have troubled hearts: a) believe in God for He will care for them. b) Jesus will one day return to be with them and c) He will take them to be with Him forever in heaven.

Isaiah 53:3 refers to Jesus as "*A man of sorrows*." Familiar with sorrow Himself, Jesus would be able to comfort the hearts of His disciples when they become sorrowful and troubled.

Many people experience troubled "hearts" in the world today. The pressures of life and broken homes are causing many hearts to be broken. The Psalmist said, "*The Lord is near to the broken-hearted and saves the crushed in spirit*" (Psalm 34:18). Jesus said, "*Peace I leave with you; my peace I give to you. Not as the world gives do I give to you. Let not your hearts be troubled, neither let them be afraid*" (John 14:27). Jesus declared that He can give peace of heart.

p 32.

He gives rest and peace of conscience

The Psalmist said, "*For my iniquities have gone over my head; like a heavy burden, they are too heavy for me*" (Psalm 38:4). Those who commit sin with apparent ease will one day have the burden of a guilty conscience to bear.

The Bible has much to say about our conscience. There is no word for "conscience" in the Old Testament Hebrew, but it is often illustrated. Joseph's brothers certainly felt the sting of their conscience when they first came to Egypt to purchase corn. While Joseph's identity was concealed, he tested his brothers, accusing them of being spies and casting them into prison. We read their response in Genesis 42:21. They said to each other, "*In truth we are guilty concerning our brother, in that we saw the distress of his soul, when he begged us and we did not listen. That is why this distress has come upon us.*" Joseph did not remind his brothers of their past cruelty and they did not know they were in his presence. Joseph wasn't dead, he was alive, and so was their conscience.

The root of the Greek word translated as 'conscience,' means 'to be aware'. The Greek speaking people in the New Testament days used this word in their everyday conversation. It basically described the pain that you feel when you do wrong. We see evidence of this in John 8:9 when those who demanded what should be done with the woman caught in the act of adultery. When Jesus wrote on the sand her accusers left one by one as their conscience convicted them and they walked away.

God as our Creator has created us as moral beings. As such, God has equipped every human being with a "built in" moral conscience. The Law was given to the Jews, but for the Gentiles their conscience bore witness to how they should live. Their conscience was like a judge and jury in their hearts. Conscience is the voice of God in the soul.

God's Word speaks of a blameless conscience and to be "blameless" means to be without offense. In Acts 24:16 Paul at his trial said, "*I always take pains to have a clear conscience towards both before God and man.*" The function of a conscience is to warn and convict us. The brothers of Joseph did not have a blameless conscience, they were filled with guilt.

God's Word also speaks of a pure or clear conscience. Paul said, "*I thank God, whom I serve, as did my ancestors, with a clear conscience, as I remember you constantly in my prayers night and day*" (2 Timothy 1:3). This is a conscience that is clean and without regret. Paul was always giving his all and doing his best for God and others.

A clear conscience is a wonderful thing and it liberates us from fear and instils courage. We can remain calm and confident even in difficult times. Proverbs 28:1 says, "*The wicked flee when no one pursues, but the righteous are bold as a lion.*" If we come to Jesus He will give us rest and peace of conscience. The conscience will no longer condemn us and we will have the peace that only Christ can give. Cf. Psalm 103:12; Isaiah 43:25; Hebrews 8:12.

He gives rest of mind and freedom from fear

A troubled mind is fertile ground for Satan to do his work. Many people struggle with anxiety or worry and cannot relax.

Anxiety is not the same thing as stress. We all experience difficulties and challenges everyday - that is stress. Anxiety is different as it develops from an anxious mindset and the feeling of restlessness and agitations when the body is uncomfortable and the mind will not slow down. Fear causes a variety of reactions depending on the intensity, timing and coping options available.

In Isaiah 26:3 we read, "*You keep him in perfect peace whose mind is stayed on you, because He trusts in you.*" Many people have a restless and troubled mind with all the worry and anxiety of the past, present and future but there is peace for those who put their trust in Christ.

Jesus told his disciples at the Last Supper, "*Let not your hearts be troubled neither let them be afraid*" (John 14:27). The book of Hebrews puts it this way, God has said, "*I will never leave you nor forsake you,*" so we say with confidence, "*The Lord is my helper, I will not fear; what can man do to me?*" (Hebrews 13:5-6).

The Lord says in Isaiah, "*Fear not, for I am with you; be not dismayed, for I am your God; I will strengthen you, I will help you, I will uphold you with my righteous right hand*" (Isaiah 41:10). God's people are told to "fear not," based on the promise God is with us and for us. We are able to "fear not" because of God's presence, power and will.

Many people are afraid of loneliness, but Christ has promised never to leave us or forsake us. Therefore, we will never be alone. Jesus has promised to be our helper and when the burden is too great for us, we have Him to help us. We can come to the Lord with our fears and receive comfort and "rest."

He gives rest for the soul

Jesus said, "*I am gentle and lowly in heart, and you will find rest for your souls*" (Matthew 11:29). Jesus alone can give us the rest we need. The real need is not so much rest for our bodies, but rest for our souls. Some have said that it is too hard to be a Christian and live for the Lord, but Jesus said His yoke is easy and His burden light.

As Christ is the only One who can give rest for the soul, it is reasonable to conclude that no true rest may be found apart from Him. We cannot by our own work or effort, create it for ourselves. It is sad to find people searching for happiness and contentment in the things of this world, or from people of this world, when all the time they do not see the need to satisfy the soul.

The Psalmist was able to say, *"The Lord preserves the simple; when I was brought low, he saved me. Return, O my soul, to your rest; for the Lord has dealt bountifully with you. For you have delivered my soul from death"* (Psalm 116:6-8).

When Jesus invited to Himself *"all you who labour and are heavy laden,"* He was speaking primarily of weariness of the soul. What makes the soul "weary and burdened"? The ultimate cause is our sin and its consequences, not to mention the impact we feel from the sin of others. However, the Psalmist was able to say, *"For God alone my soul waits in silence; from him comes my salvation, my fortress; I shall not be greatly shaken"* (Psalm 62:1-2).

The soul cannot find the rest it needs in temporal and material things. We should take time to seek God for He will bring eternal rest to the soul. After death, the souls of believers pass immediately into heaven because they have found peace with God in this life and are therefore safe and secure for eternity.

He gives rest from the temptations of Satan

The Spirit of God led Jesus into the desert to face Satan's temptations and these took place immediately after Jesus' baptism and before He began His public ministry. Why was it so important for Jesus to face these temptations from Satan?

Matthew 4:1 says, *"Then Jesus was led by the Spirit into the wilderness to be tempted by the devil."* His ministry began with testing. When God created Adam and placed him in the Garden of Eden, He tested him. He gave mankind a free will and did not make him a robot without freedom to choose for himself. The first Adam failed and we see the consequences in our lives and in this world today. Jesus, whom the Bible calls the second Adam, did not fail His test and in so doing is able to bring fallen mankind back to God to freely choose again to follow Him and His ways.

The Son of God was alone in His temptations. He had no help, support or encouragement from family or friends. Satan had Him on His own. Every follower of Christ will face a time of testing of his or her faith. The testing will usually come at the time of greatest vulnerability.

Jesus faced three temptations. The first temptation was to turn stones into bread. The second was to jump from the pinnacle of the temple in Jerusalem where He would be rescued by angels. The third temptation was to worship Satan. These temptations of Jesus were recorded to help all who are His disciples to understand how, Jesus the Son of God in flesh and blood, was *"one who in every respect has been tempted as we are, yet without sin"* (Hebrews 4:15).

We have this promise that God will never allow us to be tempted beyond our ability, and that He will always provide for us a way of escape. *"No temptation has overtaken you that is not common to man. God is faithful, and he will not let you be tempted beyond your ability, but with the temptation he will also provide the way of escape, that you may be able to endure it"* (1 Corinthians 10:13; cf. 1 John 4:4).

We should be comforted in our times of testing by the fact Jesus went through the same. Jesus meets us in our hour of need and in our moment of trial and testing, as the one who defeated evil and overcame temptation. When believers enter heaven they will no longer have to face the temptations of Satan.

He gives rest in heaven

Peter said, "*Therefore, brothers, be all the more diligent to confirm your calling and election, for if you practise these qualities, you will never fall. For in this way there will be richly provided for you an entrance into the eternal kingdom of our Lord and Saviour Jesus Christ*" (2 Peter 1:10-11). There is nothing greater to look forward to than rest in heaven. The Lord will welcome those who have come to Him as their Saviour. There is a crown waiting for those who keep the faith.

In our work we may desire security, promotion and job satisfaction; in our lives we may want excitement and pleasure but these things are only temporary. There is a future rest beyond anything that can be experienced in this life. There shall be a perfect resting from all sin in heaven, for nothing shall ever enter there which could either defile or disturb our peace.

In heaven there shall be no more sorrow from the heartache and pain of seeing the evidence and effect of sin daily in society around us. When the apostle Paul was in Athens, "*his spirit was provoked within him as he saw that the city was full of idols*" (Acts 17:16).

In heaven "*He will wipe away every tear from their eyes, and death shall be no more, neither shall there be mourning, nor crying, nor pain any more, for the former things have passed away*" (Revelation 21:4). We know that those who have put their trust in Jesus Christ to save them have the assurance of peace and rest in heaven for eternity.

Life on earth is a constant battle against the world, the flesh and the devil, but in heaven the fight will be over and life will be very different, for heaven is a place of rest.

Jesus Christ came to save sinners - those who have gone astray and come short of the glory of God. This "I will" goes right into the heart, *"whoever comes to me, I will never cast out"* (John 6:37). It does not matter who the man or woman is, or what their trials, troubles, sorrows or sins may be, Jesus gives the invitation, *"Come to me, all who labour and are heavy laden, and I WILL give you rest"* and they will truly know and experience that promised rest.

Questions for Reflection

1. What does it mean to you that Christ has promised to give 'rest'?

2. Do you think the Pharisees were too strict about keeping the Sabbath day?

3. What kind of rest does Jesus offer?

4. What are the causes for restlessness and weariness?

5. Do you agree that salvation from sin and rest from all burdens are found, not in what we do but in the person of Jesus and in Him alone?

6. If faith is all that is needed for me to get to heaven, why would I do good works?

2

"I Will" Never Leave You

"If you love me, you will keep my commandments. And I will ask the Father, and he will give you another Helper, to be with you for ever... I will not leave you as orphans; I will come to you. Yet a little while and the world will see me no more, but you will see me."
(John 14:15, 18-19)

Just before the Passover Feast, Jesus revealed to His disciples that He was not going to be on this earth much longer. We are told He *"knew that his hour had come to depart out of this world to the Father"* (John 13:1). Jesus gave the unexpected news, *"Yet a little while and the world will see me no more."* The news that Jesus was about to leave them came as a great surprise to His disciples. Who was going to be their new leader? Would the work now collapse? Could they even consider carrying on the ministry without Jesus being with them?

If Jesus should leave and never return it would be a great loss to His disciples. However, when Peter asked where He was going Jesus replied, *"Where I am going you cannot follow me now, but you will follow afterwards"* (John 13:36).

Jesus assured them that though He was leaving them, it was only for a while. He promised that He would return for His people, and that they would live with Him forever.

The Promise of someone to help us

Jesus comforted His disciples by informing them that He was not going to forget them, but would send the Helper to be with them. Notice to whom this statement was addressed. It included Peter, who would soon deny knowing Jesus, and also Thomas, who would express his doubts about Jesus' resurrection.

Jesus further explains who this Helper is and why He will come. Jesus said, *"These things I have spoken to you while I am still with you. But the Helper, the Holy Spirit, whom the Father will send in my name, he will teach you all things and bring to your remembrance all that I have said to you"* (John 14:25-26).

Jesus is describing the activity of the Holy Spirit. The Greek word used here is "Parakletos"-"para" means "alongside of," and "kletos" means "called." Taken together, the Holy Spirit is described by Jesus as "one who is called alongside of."

The King James Version translates "Parakletos" as "Comforter" because of the close connection of the English language with Latin. It is derived from the Latin word *"comfortis,"* which consisted of a prefix (*com,* meaning "with") and a root (*fortis,* meaning "strong"). It is the combination of two Latin words to mean "strength."

Today, we understand the word comfort to mean, "to be at ease and have encouragement in the time of trouble." But its original meaning was different. Originally the word carried the meaning "with strength." Therefore, the King James Version translators were telling us that the Holy Spirit comes to Christians to strengthen them in the hour of need.

Sometimes sympathy does not help or strengthen us. When someone says pleasant words and we are told to cheer up and go on - that is meaningless and does not help or give any comfort. The comfort that gives us strength comes when God sympathises with us. God gives the strength that we need. A true comforter is one who is with us in order to strengthen us.

The word *"paraklytos"* as used in John chapter 14, is a picture of one who comes alongside to help. Suppose a little girl is standing at the side of a busy road waiting for an opportunity to cross, when a friendly policeman comes, takes her by the arm and helps her across. He is one who comes alongside to help.

Surely, this is why Paul could say, *"I can do all things through him who strengthens me"* (Philippians 4:13). For Paul, the Holy Spirit was a very real Person who gave His assistance and support. Paul is saying, "In the midst of my trials, in the midst of my burdens, God came into the middle of them and strengthened me to such an extent that I was able to praise Him."

Jesus promised the Holy Spirit would come alongside to strengthen and help us and, when the Spirit is given, *"to be with you forever"* (John 14:16).

In 1 John 2:1 we are told, *"My little children, I am writing these things to you so that you may not sin. But if anyone does sin, we have an advocate with the Father, Jesus Christ the righteous."* The word translated "advocate" is the same word *"paraklytos."*

When Stephen, the first martyr, was being stoned we are told, *"But he, full of the Holy Spirit, gazed into heaven and saw the glory of God, and Jesus standing at the right hand of God"* (Acts 7:55). What a great comfort for Stephen as Jesus our "Advocate" was there to welcome him.

We are also told in Romans 8:34 how Jesus is *"at the right hand of God, who indeed is interceding for us."* As a result no accusation against us can ever be used to condemn us and no one can separate us from the love of Christ because Jesus is our "Advocate" (*paraklytos*).

Commenting on this verse, Charles Spurgeon writes, "It is a delightful truth that the Spirit of God always dwells in believers; not sometimes, but *always*... At no single moment is the Spirit of God gone from a believer."

Jesus was able to comfort His disciples and give them strength for the days that lay ahead with the words and promise, *"I will ask the Father, and he will give you another Helper, to be with you forever."* Those must have been re-assuring words for the down-hearted disciples.

Notice the careful details of what Jesus says! First, notice the word "another." The Greek language uses two words which are commonly translated "another"; *"Heteros"* and *"Allos."* The "Heteros" refers to another but of a different kind, while the "allos" refers to another of the same kind or nature. In referring to the Holy Spirit, Jesus called Him "allos" - *"another One of the same kind"*, thus stating that the Holy Spirit would be exactly like Himself. So the Holy Spirit is exactly like Jesus.

If I am using a teaspoon and ask for another spoon using *"allos"*, I am seeking another teaspoon, the same as I am using. But if you bring me a wooden spoon I might complain that I did not say *"heteros"* - another spoon of a different kind. Jesus says that the Holy Spirit is "another" Helper; and the word used is *"allos"*; that is, He is another Helper sent in place of Jesus on this earth.

The Amplified Bible translates "allos parakletos" as *"another Comforter (Counsellor, Helper, Intercessor, Advocate, Strengthener and Standby) that He may remain with you forever."* All seven words translated from the Greek "Parakletos" shows us how wide the ministry of the Holy Spirit is in our lives.

While on this earth Jesus was everything to His disciples that they ever needed. He taught them all that they needed to know. He protected them, led them, provided for them, taught them how to pray, and gave them instruction in many things. If they were confronted with a difficult situation, He solved it for them. If they were fearful, He comforted them. If they were helpless and weak, He empowered them. He was everything to them. In fact Jesus was their Comforter, Counsellor, Helper, Intercessor, Advocate, Strengthener and Standby.

Now Jesus is about to leave them, but before He goes, He promises to send another Helper who is like Him. The Holy Spirit is 'our Helper like Jesus'; who leads us where we are to go, teaches us what we need to know, and empowers us for what we need to do.

The Promise that God will never leave us

The Holy Spirit is the third person of the Trinity - Father, Son and Holy Spirit. The first thing we learn about the Holy Spirit is that He comes alongside us to strengthen us. The second is that He is always with the Christian.

Jesus says that when the Spirit is given, *"He will be with (us) forever"* (John 14:16). A few verses later, Jesus says, *"I will not leave you as orphans"* (John 14:18).

In His Sermon on the Mount Jesus promises the Father's care when He says, *"But if God so clothes the grass of the field, which today is alive and tomorrow is thrown into the oven, will he not much more clothe you, O you of little faith? Therefore do not be anxious, saying, 'What shall we eat?' or 'What shall we drink?' or 'What shall we wear?' For the Gentiles seek after all these things, and your heavenly Father knows that you need them all"* (Matthew 6:30-32).

There is no person excluded from God's care, He knows all our needs. It would be a tragedy if God knew our needs but did not care about our circumstances or was unable to do anything about them. He does care and He is able to help in each and every situation. God can provide for the personal and emotional needs in a time of loss.

Jesus had entered into the home of two sisters named Mary and Martha to comfort them upon the death of their brother Lazarus. Jesus transformed the darkness of that experience when He said, *"I am the resurrection and the life. Whoever believes in me, though he die, yet shall he live, and everyone who lives and believes in me shall never die"* (John 11:25-26).

When Jesus said *"I will never leave you"*, He was promising to come alongside, to strengthen and to always be with us. I will never leave you is a promise that has been proved many times in Scripture and in history.

a) God was with Jacob

In Genesis 28:15 we read, *"Behold I am with you and will keep you wherever you go, and will bring you back to this land. For I will not leave you until I have done what I have promised you."*

Jacob lay down to sleep with a stone for his pillow and the heavens above him, and as he slept friendless and alone, God said to him, *"I will not leave you."*

Jacob was guided to Paddan Aram and he settled there; Laban deceived him, wickedly and wrongly many times; eventually he fled with his wives and children from Laban. On the way Jacob wrestled with God seeking His blessing. Sometime later, Jacob saw Esau approaching with four hundred men, causing Jacob to divide his children among Leah, Rachel and the maidservants. However, there was a happy reunion when the two brothers met and embraced each other.

Many years later Joseph, the son of Jacob, had been sold by his brothers to the Ishmaelites. They took him to Egypt where some years later he became Governor. When Joseph's brothers came looking for food, Joseph demanded that they bring their youngest brother Benjamin, to him. Jacob was greatly upset when he was told about this, and he said to them, *"You have bereaved me of my children: Joseph is no more, and Simeon is no more, and now you will take Benjamin. All this has come against me"* (Genesis 42:36).

God had not left Jacob and many years later, as an old man, he went down to Egypt and was united with his son Joseph. God said to Jacob many years before, *"I will not leave you."* And throughout his long life God was surely with him through all his experiences to the end.

b) God was with Moses

In Deuteronomy 31:6 we read these words, *"Be strong and courageous. Do not fear or be in dread of them, for it is the Lord your God who goes with you. He will never leave you or forsake you."* Here God is speaking to a company of people through Moses. They were to drive out the giants from the Promised Land, and also the men who had chariots of iron. But the Lord said He would never leave them, which He did not do, till from Dan to Beersheba they possessed the Land. No matter what giants, opposition or difficulties we face, we can undertake any action because God has promised, *"I will never leave you or forsake you."*

Scripture provides many examples of how the presence of God enables the Christian to live for Him. One of the most powerful of these is found in the life of Moses, who was convinced that without God's presence in his life, it was useless for him to attempt anything. When he spoke face to face with the Lord, he said, "... *If your presence will not go with me, do not bring us up from here"* (Exodus 33:15). He was saying, "Lord, if your presence is not with me, then I am not going anywhere. I will not take a single step unless I am assured you are with me! "

Moses knew it was God's presence in Israel that set the people apart from all other nations, and the same is true of the church of Jesus Christ today. The only thing that sets us apart from nonbelievers is God being "with us" - leading us, guiding us, working His will in and through us.

Here is how God answered Moses' bold statement: *"...My presence will go with you, and I will give you rest"* (verse 14). What an incredible promise! The Hebrew word for "rest" is "a comfortable, quiet rest." God was saying, "No matter what enemies or trials you face, you will always be able to find a quiet rest in me!"

In spite of all the situations Moses faced with the Children of Israel, God's promise to be with him did not fail.

c) God was with Joshua

In Joshua 1:5 the Lord said to Joshua, *"No man shall be able to stand before you all the days of your life. Just as I was with Moses, so I will be with you. I will never leave you or forsake you."*

As Joshua set out to enter the Promised Land, time and time again he proved the help and strength of the Lord. There were times he would have gone back in defeat, if it were not for the faith and confidence that this promise gave him. As this promise was good for Moses and Joshua so it is an encouragement for us today. *"I will never leave you or forsake you."*

A few years ago, there was a Nigerian studying at Belfast, and when he came over he left his wife and family at home. As they had no means of income, things were very difficult financially. In Nigeria his wife was waiting for money to buy food but it did not come. Eventually all the food was finished and there was no money to buy anything for the family to eat. At night time the young children were hungry and the mother sent them to bed with an empty stomach, but assured them that tomorrow they would have something to eat for they trusted God to supply their needs.

In the morning the children got up, but there was no food, however, the mother gathered her children together and gave thanks for the food they would receive that day. Shortly after this a man arrived at their home to visit the family, who knew nothing about their need. The mother did not say anything but as he left he gave her enough money to buy food for five days. It was only some time later that the man heard what the need had been in that home, and yet they had said nothing.

Would we have faith to give thanks for food that was not there, because God promised, *"I will never leave you or forsake you?"* Surely what God said to Jacob, Moses and Joshua and in the book of Hebrews, He says to all who trust Him today.

Look at the word "*never*" in our text. It is a powerful word! God will never leave you! He will never forsake you. We cannot fully appreciate this promise nor grasp what it would be like to be forsaken of God. There is not a worse feeling than loneliness. What then would it be like if we were utterly forsaken by God?

Many thousands of people have been forsaken by family, friends and loved ones. But only one man could cry out to God to say that he was utterly forsaken by God! When on the cross bearing our sins Christ knew what it was to be forsaken by God. He cried out with a loud voice, saying, "*My God, my God, why have you forsaken me?*" (Matthew 27:46).

We can never know true happiness until we have trusted everything to Christ. Sometimes we might leave God or not live for him like we ought, but God will never leave us that is why we can say today, "The Lord is my helper." Believers are His possession. He has bought them with His own blood. God has made the promise He will never leave them!

Some reasons why God will never leave us

The Lord will not, and cannot leave His people, because of His relationship to them.

a) He is our Father

Will our heavenly Father leave us? Absolutely not! Sad to say in our society today a father will sometimes walk out of the home and leave wife and family. Jesus said, "*I will not leave you as orphans; I will come to you*" (John 14:18). There are many orphans in the world and some people may not have a good father figure in their lives, but we all have a Father who is strong and ever-present and does not disappoint us. Jesus taught us to pray to "our Father in heaven" (Matthew 6:9). He told us that when our daily needs confront us - food, clothing, shelter and protection (Matthew 6: 31) - "*your Father knows what you need before you ask him*" (v. 8).

We have a Father who is always there. Night or day, whenever the going gets tough, we can trust that He will never abandon us. He has promised to care for us and He knows better than we do what we need.

The Bible says that God is love and He wants to lavish His love on us. He wants to be in a relationship with us, not because we deserve it but because He made us, and is seeking to adopt sons and daughters for His kingdom.

While we were still alienated, God the Father made a way for us to get to heaven by sending His only Son, Jesus Christ, to earth two thousand years ago to take care of the "sin" issue that had kept us separated. In obedience to His Father, Jesus bore upon Himself the punishment for our sin on the cross.

And then again in Isaiah 49:15 we read, *"Can a mother forget her nursing child, that she should have no compassion on the son of her womb? Even these may forget, yet I will not forget you. Behold, I have engraved you on the palms of my hands; your walls are continually before me."*

The Psalmist gives us this picture, *"Father of the fatherless and protector of widows is God in his holy habitation"* (Psalm 68:5).

"I will be a Father to you, and you shall be sons and daughters to me, says the Lord Almighty" (2 Corinthians 6:18). God our heavenly Father will not forget us or leave us as orphans.

b) His honour is at stake

His honour binds Him never to forget you. In 1 Samuel 12:22 we read, *"The LORD will not forsake His people, for his great name's sake, because it has pleased the LORD to make you a people for himself."*

We are so used to politicians not keeping their campaign promises. They promise what they will do if they are elected into power but so often they fail to carry out those promises when they are actually in power.

Those broken promises hardly surprise us, but it does bother us greatly when someone we love and trust fails to keep an important promise. *"I promise to love you in sickness and in health, for richer or poorer, and to keep myself ever and only for you, till death do us part."* When those kinds of promises are broken, it leaves a trail of grief and pain.

We find God's reputation described by the term "name" in many places in the Bible. One impressive instance occurs in the record of Joshua. When Israel was defeated by the men of Ai, Joshua pleaded with the Lord. He said, *"O Lord, what can I say, when Israel has turned their backs before their enemies! For the Canaanites and all the inhabitants of the land will hear of it and will surround us and cut off our name from the earth. And what will you do for your great name?"* (Joshua 7:8-9). Joshua was concerned that God's reputation might be ruined. And so should we!

When we see a house half-built and left we say, "This man began to build and was not able to finish." But could this be said of God that He could not bring our salvation to perfection? Surely He said, *"I give them eternal life, and they will never perish, no one can snatch them out of my hand"* (John 10:28).

We are reminded that, "God is not man, that he should lie, or a son of man, that he should change his mind. Has he said, and will he not do it? Or has he spoken, and will he not fulfil it? (Numbers 23:19). God's honour is at stake when He says, *"I will never leave you nor forsake you."*

c) God loves you and will not forget about you

God loves you and He loved you before you were born, *"even as he chose us in him before the foundation of the world, that we should be holy and blameless before him. In love he predestined us for adoption as sons through Jesus Christ, according to the purpose of his will"* (Ephesians 1:4).

The most amazing truth in Christianity is that God loves us enough to seek us out even before we start trying to find him. In Luke 19:10 Jesus said, "...the Son of man (referring to himself with the term reserved for the Jewish Messiah) came to seek and to save the lost. *"For while we were still weak, at the right time Christ died for the ungodly. For one will scarcely die for a righteous person - though perhaps for a good person one would dare even to die - but God shows his love for us in that while we were still sinners, Christ died for us"* (Romans 5: 6-8).

When someone questions God's love or His care for them, all we can do is point to the cross where Jesus, His own Son, died willingly for the whole world. *"For God so loved the world, that he gave his only Son, that whoever believes in him should not perish but have eternal life"* (John 3:16). In this verse we find no conditions placed on God's love for us. God does not say, "as soon as you clean up your act, I'll love you;" nor does He say, "I'll sacrifice my Son if you promise to love Me." In fact, in Romans 5:8, we find just the opposite. God is Love, and His love is very different from human love.

God wants us to know that His love is unconditional, so He sent His Son, Jesus Christ, to die for us while we were still unlovable sinners. We did not have to clean up our lives, or make any promises to God before we could experience His love. His love for us has always existed, and because of that, He did all the giving and sacrificing long before we were even aware that we needed His love. Would someone who loves like that, then turn around and abandon the very ones He died for?

Paul reminds us, *"We are more than conquerors through him who loved us. For I am sure that neither death nor life, nor angels nor rulers, nor things present nor things to come, nor powers, nor height nor depth, nor anything else in all creation, will be able to separate us from the love of God in Christ Jesus our Lord"* (Romans 8:37-38).

Our fears for today, or worries about tomorrow or where we are - high above the sky, or in the deepest ocean - nothing will ever be able to separate us from the love of God demonstrated by our Lord Jesus Christ when He died for us.

d) God will not leave us in eternity

The apostle John wrote, *"And I heard a voice from heaven saying, 'Write this: Blessed are the dead who die in the Lord'"* (Revelation 14:13). We may say death is a bad thing; death is the great unknown, how can a voice from heaven proclaim "blessed are the dead?" Paul wrote, *"Death is swallowed up in victory. O death, where is your victory? O death, where is your sting?"* (1 Corinthians 15:54-55). Death does sting and can be very painful. Jesus Himself experienced the pain of death when His friend Lazarus died. Scripture tells us that "Jesus wept."

But here we have the answer, blessed are the dead "who die in the Lord." There are many reasons why this is the case. Death has brought relief from pain and suffering. Scripture tells us, *"He will wipe away every tear from their eyes, and death shall be no more, neither shall there be mourning nor crying, nor pain anymore, for the former things have passed away"* (Revelation 21:4).

They are also blessed because they literally see Jesus face to face. Scripture tells us that those who die in the Lord are blessed, because they will have rest from their labour. Here we have proof once again that the children of God cannot perish. The righteous are safe and secure. And of this we can be sure, the Lord will not leave nor forsake those who put their faith and trust in Him.

This is Jesus' promise of the present and ongoing ministry of the Holy Spirit in the lives of His followers on earth. What a wonderful promise this is! How important it is that we understand it!

Jesus says to all of His followers, "I will not leave you." The Holy Spirit is said to always be with the follower of Jesus. God will never leave you or forsake you. *"We are more than conquerors through him who loved us. For I am sure that neither death nor life, nor angels nor rulers, nor things present nor things to come, nor powers, nor height nor depth, nor anything else in all creation, will be able to separate us from the love of God in Christ Jesus our Lord"* (Romans 8:37-38).

What a wonderful promise we have been given for the present and the future, *"I will never leave you or forsake you."* Let us go forth with that promise to encourage us in every situation we meet.

Questions for Reflection

1. What does Jesus mean when he says, "I will never leave you"?

2. What examples from Scripture are there that Christ will not leave us?

3. Discuss some reasons why Christ will not leave us.

4. What can you say about the 'Helper' Jesus promised He would send to be with us?

5. Can you reflect on some difficult situation when you were aware of Christ's presence with you?

3
The "I Will" of Confession

"Everyone who shall confess me before men, I also will confess before My Father who is in heaven. But whoever denies me before men, I also will deny before my Father who is in heaven"
(Matthew 10:32-33)

The NIV, ESV and NRSV use the word "acknowledge", and the NASB and NKJV use the word "confess." To "acknowledge" gives the impression of a simple recognising, approving or admitting to something, whereas to "confess" generally means a positive confirming, declaring, and affirming one's faith and allegiance to Jesus Christ. Creeds and Statements of Faith are called "Confessions." That which is confessed is no longer private, but public and out in the open.

The Greek word *"homologue"* used is made up of two parts: *"homo"* which means "same" and *"loge"* which means "to speak." Therefore, it literally means "to speak the same thing as another, to agree with another person." The believer in Christ is to confess with the mouth the Lord Jesus and to vocally and publically agree with what God has said concerning His Son (Romans 10:9-10 and compare 1 John 5:9-12).

Jesus had just been explaining that two sparrows are sold for a penny (Matthew 10:29) or five sparrows sold for two pennies (Luke

12:6). However, not one of them is forgotten by God. If something so common and seemingly unimportant as a sparrow is under God's control, how much more will your Father in heaven care for you? Jesus was basically saying, "because of what I have just told you I want to assure you that you are worth more than many sparrows; indeed the very hairs of your head are all numbered" (Luke 12:7). Jesus emphasised the comfort this gives by saying, *"Fear not, therefore, you are of more value than many sparrows"* (Matthew 10:31). Jesus concludes by saying, *"So everyone who acknowledges me before men, I also will acknowledge before my Father who is in heaven"* (Matthew 10:32). He is saying, "Think about what I've just revealed to you about the Father's all-seeing, all-knowing care. Therefore, you are to confess this truth to the whole world." How then are we to confess Christ?

We are to confess Christ with our lips

When most people think of "confession," they usually think about admitting guilt, but we can also confess good things. We may confess that we love our husband or wife, our children, our country, etc.

Paul said, *"If you confess with your mouth that Jesus is Lord and believe in your heart that God raised him from the dead, you will be saved"* (Romans 10:9). True faith in the heart will lead to confessing Christ with the mouth. When Jesus visited the home of Martha and Mary before He raised their brother Lazarus from the dead, He revealed to Martha that He was *"the resurrection and the life... and whoever lives and believes in me shall never die. Do you believe that?"* Martha's reply was *"Yes, Lord, I believe that you are the Christ, the Son of God, who is coming into the world"* (John 11:27). This was Martha's confession.

The Christian can never escape the responsibility of being different from the world. We are not to be conformed to the world, but to be transformed from it. Today we live in a world where many people reject Christ and Christianity. Those who profess to know Jesus Christ as Saviour can often face difficult situations as they seek to live for Jesus. On many occasions it means to be treated as Christ was treated, and that often means, having to face a hostile world.

The apostle Paul lists two things necessary for salvation and to become a disciple of Jesus Christ. These are to confess Jesus Christ as Lord, and to believe that God has raised Him from the dead. Of course this means that part of our testimony should be that we believe that Jesus Christ satisfied God's desire for justice by taking the punishment for our sins on the cross.

Jesus Christ could not be Lord and bring us salvation from sin and the promise of eternal life, if He Himself did not overcome death, and show by His resurrection that He had been successful in paying for our sins on the cross. Belief in Jesus and His resurrection implies that we also believe that He died for our sins.

Satan is opposed to Christians, and will do everything he can to hinder our witness. It is going to cost us something to be a Christian as we live in a very indifferent world. Scripture clearly teaches that only Jesus Christ can save and we are to confess this with our mouths. We are told that if we acknowledge that we belong to Christ *"He will acknowledge you before the Father, who is in heaven."* What does that mean? That means when we are loyal enough to Jesus Christ even in difficult situations, He will speak our name in the Father's presence.

To confess Christ is to publicly and bravely acknowledge that we belong to Him. Sadly, Peter denied he was a disciple of Jesus. His reply to those who accused Him of being one of Jesus disciples was, *"I do not know the man"* (Matthew 26:72). Then he remembered what Jesus had said, *"Before the rooster crows, you will deny me three times."* Peter failed to confess his loyalty to Jesus and this convicted him greatly, resulting in him going out and weeping bitterly.

What are we to confess with our lips?

If you are standing at the side of the road and see an accident taking place then you are a witness to that accident. You have personal knowledge of it because you saw exactly what happened. The Christian has had an experience with Christ and personally knows what happened, and therefore, should be a witness for Christ.

In John 1:15 the Bible says, *"John bore witness about him."* Again John said, *"We have seen with our eyes"* (1 John 1:1). Peter and the other apostles said, *"We are his witnesses of these things"* (Acts 5:32). So the early disciples made it clear that they were witnesses of the things Jesus had done.

Occasionally, we hear of someone who had seen an accident or a social disturbance and refused to be a witness. That person did not want to be involved. Perhaps the same could be said about some Christians. They claim to have experienced Christ, to know what He has done for them, but refuse to get involved in witnessing to others.

How do people witness in a court case? They tell the court what they have seen and heard. That is all. If they add what they think, they are soon told, "we are not interested in what you think - just tell us the facts. What did you see? What did you hear?" We confess Christ in exactly the same way. Tell the facts. What has Christ done for you? What does God say in His Word? The personal testimony is unique and no one can argue against what God has done in your life.

What is it that we need to confess? We need to confess that Jesus Christ is Lord. God wants us to proclaim the same thing that Peter said, *"You are the Christ, the Son of the Living God"* (Matthew 16:16). We are to identify and acknowledge that we belong to Jesus Christ as our Saviour and Lord.

After Jesus healed a man he pleaded with Jesus to be allowed to follow Him. But Jesus said, *"Go home to your friends and tell them how much the Lord has done for you, and how he has had mercy on you"* (Mark 5:19). That is witnessing. It is not always easy. There will be those who don't want to listen, but we must remain faithful. The Apostle Paul said to Philemon, *"I pray that the sharing your faith may become effective"* (Philemon 1: 6).

We are not expected to go around boasting, but to quietly witness when the opportunity arises in our daily lives. If a person loves Jesus, he/she ought not to be ashamed to let people know it. In one way or another Christ must be confessed. We confess that no intermediary except Christ is necessary between the Christian and God in order to be absolved from sins and the assurance of eternal life in heaven.

Jesus is not talking here about a verbal acknowledgement; He is calling for a declaration of your genuine faith. "Acknowledges" is an on-going declaration of faith, not an acknowledgement or confession that happened once a long time ago.

We are to confess or acknowledge Jesus as Christ/King. Jesus prompted the disciples to state who they believed He was (Matthew 16:15-18). Peter said He was the Christ, the Son of God. "Christ" means one "anointed" to be king, ruler of God's people.

We are to confess Jesus as the Son of God. Peter declared Jesus as the Christ, the Son of the Living God (Matthew 16:16; John 1:49). Nathanael stated, *"You are the Son of God! You are the King of Israel!"*

The Samaritans met and talked with Jesus. They said they believed and knew that He was indeed the Christ, the Saviour of the world (John 4:42). Jesus is the One who died on the cross as the sacrifice for our sins. As a result, everyone can have the assurance of salvation from sin. Without Him, there would be no hope (Acts 4:12; Romans 10:9; Philippians 2:11).

We are to acknowledge Jesus as Lord. To be saved we must confess the Lord Jesus (Romans 10:9, 10). Note that this declaration is to be made with the mouth. Every Bible example of confession involves something that has been said.

Why should we confess Christ?

Mankind has a problem and the Christian knows the answer to that problem. God created man in His own image. He did not make man a robot to automatically love and obey him, but God gave man a freewill and freedom of choice.

Man chose to disobey God and go his own way. Men and women still make that choice today. This results in separation from God, for the Bible says, *"All have sinned and fall short of the glory of God"* (Romans 3:23). *"The wages of sin is death* (separation from God) *but the free gift of God is eternal life in Christ Jesus our Lord"* (Romans 6:23).

Man has tried to overcome this separation by doing good works, living a good life, being religious, but all these attempts are useless. The answer is *"For Christ also suffered once for sins, the righteous for the unrighteous, that He might bring us to God"* (1 Peter 3:18). This is why Christians need to be witnesses for Christ. They know the answer to man's problem and so need to make it known to those around them. If all Christians failed to confess Christ then no-one would know these things and be saved. Today the responsibility rests on us and if we fail then who will tell of Jesus and His love.

Part of the cost of following Jesus Christ as Lord and Saviour may result in losing many former friends. However, as a result of our bold stand for Jesus, those friends may become believers. Some people think that all that is required is to believe that Jesus Christ died for their sins and rose again from the dead to give them new life. However, the Bible makes it clear that God expects those who follow Jesus Christ to make a verbal profession of their faith in Jesus.

Paul emphasises the importance of confessing with the mouth, *"For with the heart one believes and is justified, and with the mouth one confesses and is saved"* (Romans 10:10). The Lord Jesus Christ said that out of the abundance of the heart the mouth speaks, meaning what is foremost in our hearts should come out in our speech, including our regard of Jesus Christ as Lord as well as Saviour (Luke 6:45; Matthew 12:34-37).

Where are we to confess Christ?

This confession is to be *"before men."* Therefore it is public in nature. It is the willingness to confess that Jesus is your Lord and to continue even when it may be difficult to do so. Jesus says that those who will confess Him, He will in turn confess them before the Heavenly Father.

Confessing Christ is the responsibility of all Christians in every age of the church. It is not for great occasions only, but for our daily walk through an evil world and is the duty of all believers in every rank of life. The love of Jesus Christ for us, and our love for Him, compels us to share Him with others. Jesus said, *"Whoever has my commandments and keeps them, he it is who loves me..."* (John 14:21). Jesus measures our love for Him by the extent and genuineness of our obedience to Him. As we obey, He promises He will reveal Himself to us.

Helping to fulfil the Great Commission is both a duty and a privilege. We want to honour and obey Him. We confess because He gives us a special love for others and we ought to live in such a way as to reflect His teachings.

Paul wrote, *"I count everything as loss because of the surpassing worth of knowing Christ Jesus my Lord. For his sake I have suffered the loss of all things and count them as rubbish, in order that I may gain Christ and be found in him"* (Philippians 3:8). Jesus said, *"Whoever does not take his cross and follow me is not worthy of me. Whoever finds his life will lose it, and whoever loses his life for my sake will find it"* (Matthew 10:38-39).

There are some parts of the world where there is intense persecution of Christians. However, in spite of this, many believers are publicly professing with their mouth Jesus Christ as their Lord and Saviour. Because of their courage God is blessing them individually and the Church in general. The gospel is true, it is the best news this world has ever heard.

In the history of Christianity, being a witness has carried a heavy cost. The root meaning of the word "witness" and "martyr" are the same. Therefore one can understand why many Christians today are anxious and have some reluctance about witnessing. Frequently the early witnesses for Jesus Christ in the world paid for their witness with their lives. However, when given the choice between confessing Jesus Christ as Lord of their lives and renouncing Jesus to worship the Roman gods, they were willing to die rather than deny Jesus.

Many people declare that faith is a personal matter; it is between them and God. Yet other people are uncertain of their own beliefs to be willing to share them with anyone. However, it is very important that every Christian makes a point of acknowledging Jesus Christ as Lord and Saviour.

What happens if we don't confess Christ?

Those who fail to profess Jesus before others may be more concerned with what other people think than what God thinks. It would appear that such a person does not fully understand who Jesus is and what He has done for them. Jesus says that He will not confess such a person before His Heavenly Father.

"Whoever denies me before men, I also will deny before my Father who is in heaven." The *"will deny"* demonstrates not someone who failed once, like Peter when the Lord was standing trial, but someone who is characterized by such behaviour. A true disciple who fails as Peter did will also follow his example of repentance and continue to confess Christ publicly afterward. Jesus is making

a distinction here between those who fear God and those who fear man.

To confess Christ is to publicly and boldly affirm that we belong to Him - that we are His servants and disciples. To deny Christ is to deny that He is our Master and Lord. There was an occasion when Peter denied Jesus and his response to those who accused him of being one of Jesus' disciples: *"I do not know the man"* (Matthew 26:72, 74). Peter denied that he knew Jesus specifically as his teacher and Lord.

Every believer should witness for Christ by a godly life. We make Him known by what we are and what we do. Our lives reflect on Him. Our reaction to the trials and sufferings are an opportunity to confess our faith in Him.

Failure to confess Christ may result in a loss of blessings here and a loss of reward in heaven. Therefore, the issue of confessing or denying is really one of relationship. The point is not affirming some set of facts about Jesus, though that would certainly be involved. When we confess Jesus, we will affirm His relationship to us as our Saviour.

There are those who are fearful to confess that they are followers of Jesus Christ in public because they are worried that they might go through some kind of persecution or perhaps lose their job or of being thought "odd one out." *"And do not fear those who kill the body but cannot kill the soul. Rather fear Him who can destroy both soul and body in hell"* (Matthew 10:28). The wonderful news is, *"if you confess with your mouth that Jesus is Lord and believe in your heart that God raised him from the dead, you will be saved. For with the heart one believes and is justified, and with the mouth one confesses and is saved"* (Romans 10:9-10).

However, we must not forget the "I will" promise Jesus has made - a promise He will not forget, *"Everyone who shall confess me before men, I also will confess before my Father who is in heaven, but whoever denies me before men, I also will deny before my Father who is in heaven"* (Matthew 10:32-33).

A person may think it a great honour when some victory in sport or in society has been achieved and to have their name mentioned in the Parliament of their country, or brought before the King or President. But just think what it would feel like to have our name mentioned in the kingdom of heaven by the Prince of Glory, by the Son of God, because we confessed Him here on earth.

If we are to be disciples of Jesus Christ, we have to take up our cross daily - not once a year or on the Lord's Day, but daily. And if we take up our cross and follow Him, we shall be blessed.

What are the advantages of confessing Jesus Christ?

Paul says, *"if you confess with your mouth that Jesus is Lord and believe in your heart that God raised him from the dead, you will be saved"* (Romans 10:9). In order for salvation to be complete, the sinner should publicly confess Christ as Saviour and Lord. "Believing with the heart" is insufficient in itself for eternal life. When one truly "believes with the heart," he or she will eventually "confess Jesus as Lord." This will be the evidence that genuine faith has been exercised. What takes place in the heart in faith eventually reaches the lips.

We know that acknowledging Christ as Saviour is the right thing to do. We are obeying what Jesus has told us to do. We often look at witnessing as being something that is to the benefit of the person we witness to. It is, after all, their salvation that is at stake. But, we must not forget there is a great benefit to the one who is doing the witnessing, Jesus rewards them by presenting them to his Father in heaven.

In order to be an effective witness, one needs to have a close relationship with Jesus Christ. Frequent confession of Christ before others helps remind us of our dependence on God for our own salvation. Witnessing will stimulate our spiritual growth, lead us to pray and study God's Word, and encourage us to depend on Christ. We will experience the privilege and honour of presenting Jesus to the world (2 Corinthians 5:20).

We would not take financial advice from someone who has problems managing their own money; nor would we take our motor car for repairs to someone who knows nothing about cars. This is even truer of witnessing about Jesus Christ, because we cannot influence anyone to accept Jesus Christ as their Saviour if we do not know Him ourselves.

We can share our own experiences of God - what He has done for us and through us. As we witness, our faith is strengthened - not just as we see people come to understand and accept the message of salvation, but as we see God working through us and giving us wisdom and understanding and strength to be effective witnesses.

It starts with having a personal relationship with Jesus, and letting people know of our relationship with Him. If we keep our faith to ourselves, we will essentially restrict our own spiritual growth. It is this aspect of witnessing that many people are unfortunately unaware of.

When we confess Jesus Christ we know we are doing the right thing and will experience peace of mind and will be blessed by God. Let us then rejoice in the wonderful promise that Jesus has given, "*Everyone who shall confess me before men, I also will confess before My Father who is in heaven*" (Matthew 10:32).

Questions for Reflection

1. What does it mean to confess Christ?

2. How are we to confess Christ?

3. Why should we confess Christ?

4. Where are we to confess Christ?

5. What are the rewards in confessing Christ?

4
The "I Will" of Cleansing

(Matthew 8:1-4; Mark 1:40-44; Luke 5:12-14)

"While Jesus was in one of the cities, there came a man full of leprosy. And when he saw Jesus, he fell on his face and begged him, 'Lord, if you will, you can make me clean.' And Jesus stretched out his hand and touched him, saying, 'I will; be clean.' And immediately the leprosy left him."

(Luke 5:12-13)

We all know how important it is to wash our hands when working with food and how hospital wards are supplied with antiseptic hand gel which medical staff and visitors use before they see patients.

The routine of "scrubbing up" by surgeons before an operation is, of course, a well-established practice, but this was not always the case. Until the late 1800s surgeons did not scrub up before surgery or even wash their hands between patients, causing infections to be transferred from one patient to another.

Ignaz Philipp Semmelweis, a Hungarian doctor working in an obstetric hospital in Vienna, made the important discovery in 1847, that hand washing with chlorinated lime solutions reduced the frequency of fatal puerperal or "childbed" fever. Deaths were reduced considerably and Semmelweis became known as the "saviour of the mothers".

Other doctors rejected Semmelweis' arguments and he was dismissed from the hospital and afterwards had difficulty, as a medical doctor, getting employment. Today, Semmelweis is considered a pioneer of antiseptic procedures, due to his discovery of the value of hand washing.

Leprosy starts by damaging the small nerves on the skin's surface resulting in a loss of sensation. The disease attacks the nervous system and if it is not noticed, gradually the victim is unable to feel pain. Those with leprosy could step on a stone or a thorn and injure their feet but not know there was a problem until they become infected and ulcerous. The person with leprosy could lift a stick fallen out of the fire, or lift a hot pot, or use scalding water to wash dishes or clothes and not realise that they have burned or scalded their hands. Also a piece of grit or dust may enter the eye and the person would not feel it, which could result in becoming blind. Without feeling pain, people injure themselves and the injuries can become infected, resulting in tissue loss.

Some years ago at a Bible College in Nigeria a student spoke to the Principal about a small patch on his face. He was advised to go to the hospital and there it was confirmed he had leprosy. Thankfully because it was detected early, he was cured and one year later was able to return to complete his studies

If left untreated, leprosy will damage the large nerves in the body resulting in the loss of sensation in the hands and feet and muscle paralysis which causes clawed fingers and foot drop. These can be difficult to heal and the infection often results in the hands and feet being deformed, with the shortening of fingers and toes ultimately leading to the amputation of limbs. Therefore, the person suffering from leprosy cannot hide the disease as it progressively gets worse.

The man with leprosy came to Jesus

In these passages of scripture (Matthew 8:1-4; Mark 1:40-44; Luke 5:10-14) we read about a man who had leprosy. He was a man with a deadly skin disease and had been separated from his family and from society because of this contagious disease.

The consequences of leprosy

In both the Old and New Testaments of the Bible, the word "leprosy" is a broad term which includes a wide range of skin diseases. The very worst of these is what we know as 'leprosy' today - a condition which is also called "Hansen's Disease." It was not only alarming in itself, it was also considered to be a curse from God.

The consequences were far more serious than just being physical. With years of suffering and disfigurement ahead, as well as the possibility of an early death, those with leprosy were boycotted by Jewish law.

A person who had leprosy should not be seen in public, because the Law of Moses stated that those who had leprosy were to stay in a special camp away from people until the leprosy disappeared from their bodies.

The Mosaic Law prescribed that the person be cut off from society, including his family. He had to wear torn clothing, have his head uncovered and let his hair be unkempt. Wherever he went he was to warn others to keep their distance and shout *"Unclean! Unclean!"* (Leviticus 13:45). Obviously this man had a great need and was in a desperate and helpless situation.

The worst fact of all was that there was nothing and no one who could help him. Moses and the Law could not help this man. The Law could tell him that leprosy was bad - where he had to live, how he had to dress, and what he had to shout - but it could not cure him. He could make every sacrifice in the book of Leviticus, but he would still have leprosy.

There was no doctor in Jerusalem or Galilee who could prescribe anything to make him better. Leprosy at that time was an incurable disease. Luke, the doctor, tells us this man was *"full of leprosy."* It could have affected his face, hands and feet and he could have been covered with a mass of ulcers and sores. His disease possibly was at an advanced stage.

The man with leprosy comes to Jesus for cleansing

In spite of his terrible circumstances, this man with leprosy came to Jesus. He may be forgiven if he had hesitated about coming as his leprosy prevented him from entering the cities where Jesus taught, or to be with the crowds that saw His miracles. Yet as a result of what he heard, he came to Jesus and believed that if Jesus was willing, He could make him clean.

No one with leprosy would have come near an orthodox scribe or rabbi for fear of being stoned but this man came to Jesus. He must have heard of Jesus' many miracles of healing, so in desperation he risked possible flogging by approaching Jesus. He had confidence in Jesus' willingness to welcome a man with leprosy that any other person would have driven away. Therefore, no one should feel unable to approach Jesus with their concerns and problems.

This man wanted to be cleansed not just healed. It is important that this man, who was unclean does not simply say to Jesus "heal me", but rather he says, "make me clean". On the surface those two statements may seem to be the same but they are not. While it is true that this man's disease had caused him a great deal of physical distress, it was his uncleanness which had separated him from God's people. A person with leprosy was excluded from the sacrifices, religious festivals and worship services. In many ways, he was not only separated from God's people, he was separated from God.

Therefore, if he were to be healed, he still had to go to the priest and carry out an extensive ritual of cleansing before he could be accepted back into the religious community and worship. It is hardly surprising that one of this man's strongest desires was to be cleansed so that he could once again worship with the people of God. This man wanted to worship God and Jesus gave him the ability to do so.

The man with leprosy asked if Jesus would cleanse him

This man demonstrated great faith when he said, "*Lord, if you are willing you can make me clean*" (v.12). That is all that mattered to him. The man with leprosy didn't doubt Jesus' power to heal, the question was would Jesus be willing to heal him?

Early in Jesus' ministry He said to the people in His own local synagogue in Nazareth, "*there were many lepers in Israel in the time of the prophet Elisha, and none of them was cleansed, but only Naaman the Syrian*" (Luke 4:27). In Israel there were hundreds of people with leprosy amongst God's chosen people, the Jews, yet it was Naaman, a Gentile from Syria, who was chosen to be cleansed showing that the option of mercy is with God alone.

The man with leprosy believed that Jesus had the power to make him clean, but was He willing? He did not take for granted that God would show mercy on him, "*when he saw Jesus, he fell on his face and begged him, 'Lord, if you are willing, you can make me clean.'*" He was supposed to shout, "*Unclean!*" to keep Jesus away, but he rejected the customs and ignored the consequences to meet Jesus.

It must have been a great shock to those around them to see the reaction of Jesus. "*Jesus stretched out his hand and touched him, saying, 'I will; be clean.' And immediately the leprosy left him.*" That would have been a wonderful experience for this man and to those who witnessed what happened. Let us follow the example of this man in whatever need we have, we can bring it to the Saviour.

Jesus was "willing" to cleanse the man with leprosy

There was no doubt in this man's mind that Jesus had the ability to heal him, if He was willing. We are told, *"Moved with pity, he stretched out his hand and touched him and said to him, 'I will; be clean.'"*

Is it God's will to heal everyone?

There are those who teach that God will heal everyone from every physical ailment as long as they have faith and believe. They would maintain that it is a lack of faith to pray, "If it be your will, heal me," but simply claim that the healing should take place.

However, this man came to Jesus and said, *"If you are willing, you can make me clean."* Does this suggest something of awareness on the man's part of a divine purpose there may have been in his affliction? Jesus did not rebuke him or tell him he had approached Him in the wrong way, or that he ought to claim his healing. In fact, we never find this idea in Scripture.

The Scriptures are clear that sometimes it is in God's will that sickness has come upon us. Not that this is how God planned things when He created humanity, but that given the circumstances in which we now live and the fallen nature of humanity, there are times when God's will for His children is to pass through physical affliction.

Paul came before the Lord and asked three times for the removal of a *"thorn in the flesh"*. We do not know what the nature of this affliction was but the Lord said to him, *"My grace is sufficient for you"* (2 Corinthians 12:7-9). Paul understood that God wanted him to learn to live with the problem he had by the grace of God. So it is clear that it is not the teaching of Scripture that everybody would be healed.

On another occasion Jesus and His disciples saw a man blind from birth. He was asked *"Rabbi, who sinned, this man or his parents, that he was born blind?"* Jesus answered, *"It was not that this man sinned, or his parents, but that the works of God might be displayed in him"* (John 9:2-3).

Lazarus became ill and died. Jesus said, *"it is for the glory of God"* (John 11:4). Later, He also told His disciples it was for their benefit so that they may believe (John 11:15).

That we would be healed from all illness is our desire, but the reality is that even in Jesus' time, healing was not always a reality. When God wanted to do something special and significant, He healed. At other times, sickness was a trial or a way of life, but in all instances, God's grace was sufficient (2 Corinthians 12:9-10).

We must not presume upon God's healing, though we ought to believe in it. God does heal even today, but it is because He wants to (James 5:13-16). He honours the prayers of faith but He doesn't always answer in the way we would like. Some believers firmly believe God will heal, but on occasions the Almighty and wise God has chosen not to heal.

Yet there are also many testimonies where doctors have been amazed by the miraculous healing of some people. Regardless of what God decides to do, we can trust that His way and will is best. We cannot compel God to heal, but we can ask and believe if it is His will, to do so. Jesus did not heal everyone. At the pool of Bethesda Jesus found, *"a multitude of invalids – blind, lame, and paralyzed"* (John 5:3). Yet, after healing only one man, *"Jesus had withdrawn, as there was a crowd in the place"* (John 5:13). He could have healed everyone, but as recorded in John chapter 9, He chose to heal only one person, and this, for the glory of God.

God causes all things to work for our good, even sickness or death. As Paul said, *"to live is Christ, and to die is gain"* (Philippians 1:21). One day sickness will not be an issue, but until we are with Jesus, let us pray for healing and grace to endure all things.

God is sovereign. He decides who is healed and who is not, who lives and who dies, who is exalted and who is humbled. We must accept by faith the idea God knows what our needs are better than we know. Jesus does not rebuke this man with leprosy for stating the qualifying phrase – "*Lord, if you are willing?*" In fact, He accepts the statement when He says, "*I will; be clean.*" He was saying the time has come for the healing to occur. Whatever purpose the leprosy may have served, it had been accomplished, and the time had come for the man to be healed.

Jesus was willing to heal the man with leprosy

Jesus did the unthinkable for this man. No doubt the disciples and those standing nearby were alarmed and shocked when they saw Jesus stretching out His hand and touch this man with leprosy. Mark tells us, "*Moved with pity, he stretched out his hand and touched him*" (Mark 1:41). This man was "covered with leprosy" and therefore an unpleasant sight. However, our Lord was always filled with compassion toward those who were suffering and oppressed.

Jesus could have shown no compassion or emotion towards this unclean man. However, only the compassionate Jesus would touch this helpless man and perform such a great act of mercy to him. By touching him Jesus showed His divine character.

The touch of Jesus was an outward and visible sign of the inward invisible compassion in the heart of the Lord. He wanted this man to know His willingness to heal him, and His infinite sympathy for him. It would have been quite possible for our Lord to heal this man by a word alone; there was no need to touch him.

Jesus showed His power, for we are told, "*And immediately the leprosy left him*" (Luke 5:13). This man was covered with leprosy and sores, and in an instant he was free from the disease that troubled him.

Matthew 8:1-15 records three miracles that Jesus performed. This man with leprosy was healed with a touch (v1-4); a centurion's servant was healed with a word – Jesus did not meet him (v 5-13); and Peter's mother-in-law was healed with a touch (v14-15).

The circumstances of the three cases were all different. The man with leprosy knelt before Him and said, *"Lord, if you will, you can make me clean."* There was the centurion's servant who was ill and Jesus said He would go and heal him, but the centurion said, *"Lord, I am not worthy to have you come under my roof, but only say the word, and my servant will be healed"* (Matthew 8:8).

Later Jesus went to Peter's house whose mother-in-law lay in bed with a fever. Jesus *"touched her hand, and the fever left her, and she rose and began to serve him"* (Matthew 8:15). In each case the heart of the Lord Jesus was one and the same. In each case He was quick to show mercy and ready to heal.

Sin has similarities to leprosy

Leprosy is an illustration of sin. It starts as an invisible infection and then slowly dominates one's life. The biblical point of view is that this is the problem with the human race. The instructions given to the priest in Leviticus 13 about infectious skin diseases can also be said about sin. Sin is deeper than the skin (Leviticus 13:3); It spreads (Leviticus 13:8); it defiles a person and can cause other people to stay away from them (Leviticus 13:45-46).

Leprosy often starts as a little spot, showing the beginning of something that was working underneath the skin, and would soon be clearly seen as it develops. Similarly, we need to be watchful of the little things in everyday life, the issues that seem so unimportant – the lie, the pride, the lustful glance, the bit of gossip. These may seem too small to bother about, but Scripture says, *"how great a forest is set ablaze by such a small fire!"* (James 3:5). Some apparently insignificant incident develops into a habit which one knows is not right, but it grows and grows until at last sin is exposed.

Leprosy is a terrible disease and sin is also extremely serious. It is the one thing which has afflicted the whole universe, broken millions of hearts and brought dishonour to God, the One who created the world and every human being in it.

Jesus did not come into the world to heal the physically sick, His mission was to *"seek and to save the lost"* spiritually (Luke19:10). He did not want people to come to Him just to be healed physically; He wanted to heal them spiritually of their sin sickness.

There is no 'human' cure for sin

Humanly speaking this man had no hope of a cure. Doctors may have taken his money and given all sorts of medicine and made many promises but they couldn't cure him. He had no hope apart from a miraculous cure through Jesus. Leprosy was an incurable disease in Jesus' day, and sin cannot be cured by human efforts. No cure has been invented but the divine one – the mighty power of the gospel of the Lord Jesus Christ.

People may make resolutions and promises to change. Some of the wisdom of the world may help us learn to get along better with others, but none of it can reconcile us to the Holy God whose law we have broken. We can deny our sin and guilt and tell ourselves that it is not there, but it *is* and there is no human way to remove it.

We are told about the result of Jesus' touch. The literal translation is *"And immediately departed from him the leprosy, and he was cleansed"* (Mark 1:42). There are *two* results: Jesus *"heals the disease"* and He *"cleanses the leper"*. These are two separate results, not two ways of saying the same thing.

The Bible considers healing and cleansing as two separate acts. Therefore, this is not an example of Jesus only healing physically. By cleansing the man with leprosy, Jesus was providing spiritual healing as well as physical healing.

This man did not get dressed up in clean clothes and try to make a good appearance, seeking to hide the horrible sores and disfigurement that covered his body before coming to Jesus. He went to Jesus with the visible evidence of his disease and appealed for cleansing. Jesus immediately reached out and touched him and said *"Be Clean"*, and every trace of the disease disappeared.

Sometimes people think that they have to "clean up their lives" before God will accept them, but that is not what we see in Scripture. When speaking to the woman at the well who was living with a man to whom she was not married, Jesus addressed the fact of her sin, then offered her the salvation she needed (John 4:1-26). Again, when another woman who had been caught in the act of adultery was brought before Jesus, He told her, *"go, and from now on sin no more."* (John 8:1-11).

Sin is never excused or ignored, but forgiveness is offered to anyone who recognizes the truth of their sin and is willing to confess and forsake it. While God certainly expects us to leave our sin, that comes as a part of our salvation, not as a precondition; we are not able to clean ourselves up without God's help.

Christ can cleanse the sinner and give salvation

This man was instantly and totally healed, so the sinner who trusts in Christ is immediately cleansed and reconciled to God. God is gracious, loving, and forgiving, calling us to salvation, even though we don't deserve it. While we were still sinners, Christ died for us (Romans 5:8), making it possible for us to receive forgiveness and cleansing from sin.

When Jesus gave the word, the man with leprosy was cleansed of all his leprosy and when Jesus saves lost sinners, they are cleansed of all their sins, and are spiritually healed. Jesus never fails to save those who call upon him. *"He is able to save to the uttermost those who draw near to God through him, since he always lives to make intercession for them"* (Hebrews 7:25).

In New Testament days, because of the fear of being infected, it was at great personal risk for anyone to touch someone with leprosy. Therefore, we could say that when Jesus touched this man, He received his uncleanness, but He also transmitted His health to the unclean man. In a similar way this is what Jesus did for us on the cross, He bore the punishment for our sins and we are justified through Him (2 Corinthians 5:21).

The man with leprosy did not question Jesus ability to heal, but asked if He was willing to heal him. Similarly, God is willing to save. God *"is not slow to fulfil his promise as some count slowness, but is patient toward you, not wishing that any should perish, but that all should reach repentance"* (2 Peter 3:9). He *"desires all people to be saved and to come to the knowledge of the truth"* (I Timothy 2:3-4).

Jesus became familiar with our grief when He took upon Himself the sinner's guilt and penalty for sin. Jesus shared this man's plague when He put forth His hand and touched him.

The reason Jesus had to die for our sins was that we could be forgiven and go to be with the Lord. Jesus is God in flesh (John 1:1, 14; Colossians 2:9), and only God can satisfy the Law requirements of a perfect life and perfect sacrifice that cleanses us of our sins.

The prophet Isaiah said, *"He was pierced for our transgressions; he was crushed for our iniquities: upon him was the chastisement that brought us peace, and with his wounds we are healed. All we like sheep have gone astray; and we have turned – everyone – to his own way; and the LORD has laid on him the iniquity of us all"* (Isaiah 53:5-6). All people have sinned against God. God is infinitely holy and righteous and therefore He must punish the sinner.

The punishment for sin is death - separation from God. Therefore, as sinners we need a way to escape the righteous judgement of God. That is why Jesus is God in flesh. He is both divine and human. He was made under the Law (Galatians 4:4), and He fulfilled it perfectly. Therefore, His sacrifice to God the Father on our behalf is of infinite value and is sufficient to cleanse all people from their sins. *"For God so loved the world, that he gave his only Son, that whoever believes in him should not perish but have eternal life"* (John 3:16).

The two words *"I will"* are very significant. Throughout Scripture we find many "I will's" of Jesus. God 'will' have mercy on whom He wants to have mercy (Romans 9:18). God 'will' cleanse from sin those who call upon Him. Every sinner that comes to Jesus for salvation He 'will' save, and He 'will' in no wise cast them out!

Questions for Reflection

1. Why did the man with leprosy ask Jesus if He was willing to cleanse him?

2. Should we expect God to heal everyone who is sick?

3. In what ways can we compare sin with leprosy?

4. Who can cleanse us from sin?

5. What did the man with leprosy do to be cleansed, and what does a sinner need to do to be cleansed from sin?

5
The "I Will" of Salvation

*"This is the WILL of my Father, that everyone who looks on
the Son and believes in him should have eternal life,
and I WILL raise him up on the last day."*
(John 6:40)

When Joseph and Mary brought the baby Jesus to the temple, Simeon took Him in his arms, blessed God and said, *"Lord, now you are letting your servant depart in peace, according to your word; for my eyes have seen your salvation that you have prepared in the presence of all peoples"* (Luke 2:29-31).

Paul said, *"Christ Jesus came into the world to save sinners"* (1Timothy 1:15). Jesus said, *"The Son of Man came to seek and to save the lost"* (Luke 19:10). In the book of Acts we read, *"There is salvation in no one else, for there is no other name under heaven given among men by which we must be saved"* (Acts 4:12). God's salvation is in a Person, and that Person is God's only Son.

Why do we need salvation?

In Genesis 1:26-27 we read, *"Then God said, "Let us make man in our image, after our likeness, ...So God created man in his own image, in the image of God he created him; male and female he created them."*

Man was created a unique being in the likeness of God. However, when Adam and Eve were tested in the Garden of Eden they failed and disobeyed God (Genesis 3:1-19). In denial of God's Word they disobeyed God's command when they followed Satan's suggestion. As soon as they had eaten the forbidden fruit they became sinners and could not return to the sinless state in which they were created.

They were cast out of the Garden of Eden and their sin led to separation from God (spiritual death). Sin is rebellion against God. It is about rejecting God's way. In 'The Shorter Catechism of the Westminster Assembly of Divines' the question is asked (no. 17): "Into what estate did the fall bring mankind"? The answer given is "The fall brought mankind into an estate of sin and misery". This is a very clear statement of what has happened to mankind as a result of sin coming into the world through Adam. This is supported by the apostle Paul, *"Therefore, just as sin came into the world through one man, and death through sin, and so death spread to all men because all sinned"* (Romans 5:12). Sin is the reason why we are out of step with God and why we are without hope in the world.

Our first parents disobeyed God's command and sin entered God's perfect world and had a devastating effect upon it. God said to Adam, *"Because you have listened to the voice of your wife and have eaten of the tree of which I commanded you, 'You shall not eat of it,' cursed is the ground because of you; in pain you shall eat of it all the days of your life"* (Genesis 3:17). After Adam and Eve were expelled from the Garden children were born to them, who were born in their likeness - sinners by nature. We are told that Adam *"fathered a son in his own likeness, after his image, and named him Seth"* (Genesis 5:3). Therefore, all Adam's descendants are born in his likeness to his sinful nature.

Humanity has a serious problem which we are incapable of dealing with ourselves. Every human effort since the 'fall' toward restoring fellowship with God has not been successful. The curse of sin follows the sinner into the next life for those who die in their sins (John 8:24). However, God is a God of mercy and of grace and He gave Adam and Eve the promise of the coming Seed of the woman. He was to bruise the head of Satan (Genesis 3:15). The promise of a Saviour was given.

Christ sacrificed His life for mankind

God was moved to deal with the problem of sin because He loves humanity. God so loved the world that he sent His Son who dealt with sin by dying on the cross. The only solution to our problem is Jesus Christ.

Before Jesus was born, an angel came to Joseph and said, *"Joseph, son of David, do not fear to take Mary as your wife, for that which is conceived in her is from the Holy Spirit. She will bear a son, and you shall call his name Jesus, for he will save his people from their sins"* (Matthew 1:20-21). This birth was not of the flesh, it was by the power of the Holy Spirit. Just as we did not bring about our own human birth, we cannot generate our own spiritual birth.

Jesus said that He was "sent" by the Father. It wasn't an accident or a coincidence that Jesus came. God had a pre-determined purpose in sending His Son. *"But when the fullness of time had come, God sent forth his Son, born of woman, born under the law, to redeem those who were under the law, so that we might receive adoption as sons"* (Galatians 4:4-5).

Jesus came to save His people from their sins. He lived on this earth for over thirty years facing all sorts of opposition from man and from Satan, and yet He was able to "finish" what He had come to do on the cross. *"It is finished"* are the last recorded words of Christ before His death (John 19:30). It is evident that He was not referring to His life, service or suffering; but rather to a special work which His Father had given Him to do. This work did not begin until He was on the cross and was completed when He died.

Christ died so that we might live for all eternity. What He did does not need to be repeated. It is something accomplished for every person and in such perfection as to be fully satisfied to the infinite God. The offense of sin had separated the sinner from God, yet God provided His own Lamb to bear away the sin forever. The holy judgments of God were against the sinner because of his sin, yet Christ became the propitiation for the sin of the whole world.

Almost every passage relating to the cross proclaims the divine reason for the sacrifice of Christ. He died as a substitute for someone else, and that someone is each and every individual in all the lost world of mankind. *"But he was pierced for our transgressions; he was crushed for our iniquities; upon him was the chastisement that brought us peace, and with his stripes we are healed. All we like sheep have gone astray; we have turned - every one - to his own way; and the LORD has laid on him the iniquity of us all"* (Isaiah 53:5-6).

Jesus said, *"For this reason the Father loves me, because I lay down my life that I may take it up again. No one takes it from me, but I lay it down of my own accord. I have authority to lay it down, and I have authority to take it up again. This charge I have received from my Father"* (John 10:17-18). Jesus makes it clear that no one took His life from Him. He made no resistance to His crucifixion, which must have been in sharp contrast to the violent struggles and cursing of the two thieves who were crucified with Him. So the last words recorded as coming from His lips on the cross were of victory and authority. *"Father, into your hands I commit my spirit!"* (Luke 23:46).

The soldiers may have crucified Christ on the cross, but only God could accomplish what He set out to do by the sacrificial death of His Son. *"For our sake he made him to be sin who knew no sin, so that in him we might become the righteousness of God"* (2 Corinthians 5:21). Jesus Christ 'knew no sin'. He lived on this earth and did not commit sin. He was able to say, *"Which one of you convicts me of sin?"* (John 8:46). Jesus sacrificed His life and was our sinless substitute on the cross.

God has a plan for all mankind

God alone could solve the problem of man's sin. In eternity past, He ordained His divine plan which centred in His divine Son; *"For God so loved the world that he gave his only Son, that whoever believes in him should not perish but have eternal life"* (John 3:16).

There are a number of references in Scripture to show how God had a plan for every human being from the beginning of time and before we were born: Jeremiah 1:5; I Corinthians 2:7; Galatians 1:15; Ephesians 1:3-4, 5, 9. God is all knowing of the past, present and future.

The reason why any man or woman has been called and saved by God is not because of their goodness, but because of God's own purpose and His unmerited grace in eternity past. Paul says that God is the one, *"who saved us and called us to a holy calling, not because of our works but because of his own purpose and grace, which he gave us in Christ Jesus before the ages began"* (2 Timothy 1:9). John's vision in Revelation tells us that the individual whose name was written in the book of life was determined, *"from the foundation of the world"* (Revelation 17:8).

Salvation comes by the grace of God with no consideration of merit or good works by man (Ephesians 2:8-9). Before Adam's fall he had the ability to respond to good or evil. He was created with the potential to sin; however, God neither created man sinful nor encouraged him to sin (Genesis 2:16-17). The ability to respond to evil was not sinful, but when Adam responded in an act of disobedience under Satan's influence, he sinned.

No one can respond positively to the gospel without the influence or conviction of the Spirit of God (John 3:5; 16:8). If a man or woman responds positively to the Spirit's influence that person experiences salvation. If they respond negatively in unbelief, they continue to be in a lost state. It is important to acknowledge that the doctrine of election does not in any way restrict offering the gospel freely to all. Whoever believes in Jesus will have eternal life (John 3:16).

God has declared that not a single one of those He has saved by His grace will ever be lost! God sent Jesus here to die so that those who look to Him by faith for salvation would have the guarantee of eternal life - that is His plan.

Chosen by God

Peter started his first letter by addressing it to, *"those who are elect exiles of the dispersion"* (1 Peter 1:1). Peter is seeking to encourage Christians who are being mistreated and persecuted for their faith by sharing with them how special they are to God. He starts his message by saying they are "elect".

Election is often a controversial doctrine among Christians, but here it is given as an encouragement. He talks about what happens to those who are 'elect' and how each person of the triune God is involved in their salvation. God the Father elects them, the Son dies to save them and the Holy Spirit sanctifies them. Therefore believers are special among the people of the world.

Election (choosing) represents a great Biblical truth. While the act of election according to God's foreknowledge occurred in eternity past, the salvation of any individual requires a personal response by faith. Remember this doctrine is part of God's inspired Word, which is for our spiritual benefit. *"All Scripture is breathed out by God and profitable for teaching, for reproof, for correction, and for training in righteousness, that the man of God may be competent, equipped for every good work"* (2 Timothy 3:16-17).

When Jesus addressed His disciples in John 15:16, He said, *"You did not choose me, but I chose you."* When Jesus told His disciples that they had not chosen Him, He did not say they never made a decision to become His followers; but rather if Jesus had not first called them and given them the opportunity to respond they would not have made the choice.

Paul says God *"chose us in him before the foundation of the world, that we should be holy and blameless before him. In love he predestined us for adoption to himself as sons through Jesus Christ, according to the purpose of his will, to the praise of his glorious grace."* (Ephesians 1:4-6).

Therefore, election is a cause for comfort and for assurance that God will work for our good today. This will happen 'not because of our works' but because of God's own purpose and grace, which he gave us in Christ Jesus before the ages began' (2 Timothy 1:9).

While we may not understand election, predestination and individual accountability, they are all taught in scripture. As C.H. Spurgeon said on one occasion, "If you try to explain election, you will lose your mind; but if you try to explain it away, you will lose your soul." H.A. Ironside said, "You may say you do not believe in election or predestination. Then you will have to tear a number of pages out of your Bible, for there are many of them which magnify God's sovereign electing grace." Scripture says, *"For those whom he foreknew he also predestined to be conformed to the image of his Son, in order that he might be the firstborn among many brothers"* (Romans 8:29).

A person needs to be 'Born Again'

In the life, death and resurrection of the Lord Jesus Christ, God has provided the perfect answer to man's greatest need. Jesus said to Nicodemus, a learned Jewish leader, and a member of the Sanhedrin council of the Jews which ruled in religious matters, *"Truly, truly, I say to you, unless one is born again he cannot see the kingdom of God."* And again He said, *"Do not marvel that I said to you, 'You must be born again'"* (John 3:3, 7).

Nicodemus said to Him, *"How can a man be born when he is old? Can he enter a second time into his mother's womb and be born?"* (John 3:3-4). It is obvious that Jesus is not talking about being born a second time physically as Nicodemus implied. Then what does the rebirth mean? Jesus said that we should not marvel at this statement. However, it is the most marvellous thing in the whole world that we mortal beings should have the offer and opportunity of becoming sons and daughters of the Almighty and Eternal God (John 1:12).

Nicodemus came by night to Jesus and called him "Rabbi" and admitted that Jesus was "a teacher come from God". Without any preliminaries Jesus sternly told this great moral and religious leader that it would be impossible for him to see the kingdom of God without being born again. Here Jesus made it clear to Nicodemus that no one in all the world can ever see God without the miraculous change of heart, that of being born again. *"Do not marvel that I said to you, 'You MUST be born again.'"* It could not be more clear and explicit, it is impossible for any person, anywhere, to see the kingdom of God or enter heaven without a new birth.

It is clearly taught in scripture that because of the sin of Adam the whole human race fell and became sinners, every child ever born is tainted with a disposition to sin. The Jews believed on physical circumcision and keeping of the ceremonial laws to get them to heaven, and many people believe that being baptized as a child, having their name on a church record book and living a good life is good enough to get to heaven, but Jesus made it clear to Nicodemus that he must be born again.

Down through the years many people have thought that being a Christian, being a child of God, depended on living a certain kind of life, going through rites and ceremonies, but that is not true. People are not Christians by trying to do things for God. The only way to be a Christian, to be saved, to be a child of God, is to receive a new heart and a new nature from God.

Paul said, *"I am a Jew, born in Tarsus in Cilicia, but brought up in this city, educated at the feet of Gamaliel according to the strict manner of the law of our fathers, being zealous for God as all of you are this day, I persecuted this Way to the death, binding and delivering to prison both men and women..."* (Acts 22:2-5). Yet Paul needed a conversion experience (Acts 9:1-22).

In the conversation with Nicodemus Jesus gives further explanation on this new birth. *"That which is born of the flesh is flesh, and that which is born of the Spirit is spirit"* (John 3:6). Every person born of human parents is sinful; therefore, every person must receive a new nature from God spiritually if they are to enter the kingdom of Heaven. No one can become a Christian until they are born of the Spirit.

The only way for a child to become part of a family is to be born or adopted into the family. They are not children of a family because they did something for the father or mother. We can be God's child only when we are born again and given spiritual life by God.

Nicodemus was surprised at the teaching of Jesus, how could he, a grown man and a Pharisee, be born again. But Jesus explained that the new spiritual birth is a miracle, just as the physical birth is a miracle.

How can a person be born again?

How does one receive the new birth and know they are born again? That is what Nicodemus wanted to know and so Jesus explained it to him in John 3:14-21. Jesus reminds Nicodemus about what happened to the Israelites when they rebelled against Moses. God sent snakes among the people to bite them and many died. When the people began to die Moses prayed for them and God told Moses to make a brass snake and put it upon a pole in the middle of the camp and whoever looked at the brass snake would immediately be healed and not die of snake bite.

Those bitten by a snake, no matter where they were in the camp, had only to look at the brass snake on the pole and they would become well. Similarly Jesus Christ was lifted on a cross, bearing our sins and all we have to do is to look to Jesus and we will receive everlasting life. *"For God so loved the world, that he gave his only Son, that whoever believes in him should not perish but have eternal life"* (John 3:16). As the chorus puts it, "He paid a debt He did not owe, I owed a debt I could not pay, I needed someone to wash my sins away."

We have all turned away from God, gone our own way, made our own decisions and pleased ourselves (Isaiah 53:6); this is why we need to repent and turn from sin, change our mind and will. From the Lord's words we know that to enter into God's kingdom, we must repent of our sins and confess to Him (Matthew 4:17; Luke 13:3). Therefore, the new birth can only be received one way; we must repent, confess our sins, turn to Jesus Christ and trust Him to do for us what we cannot do for ourselves.

Repentance is not simply remorse or regret. Judas confessed with deep remorse: "I have sinned by betraying an innocent man to death." Yet, instead of repenting and turning to God, he turned on himself, and committed suicide. True repentance will cause us to confess and forsake our sins (Proverbs 28:13). A change of mind will result in a change of course, or direction in life.

Peter said, *"Repent you therefore, and be converted, that your sins may be blotted out"* (Acts 3:19). When we do something wrong in the sight of God, this is called sin. No one is perfect, *"For all have sinned and fall short of the glory of God"* (Romans 3:23). We need to repent of our sins and seek God to forgive us and cleanse us from all sin.

Jesus said, *"Whoever comes to me I will never cast out"* (John 6:37) - what a great offer that is. What a great promise. It has no restrictions. It tells us that anyone is welcome to come in any way at any time. Salvation comes totally from the grace of God with no merit of good works by man (Ephesians 2:8-9). God has provided a full and complete salvation from sin for everyone who trusts in His Son (John 1:29; Hebrews 10:14). The Lord gave Himself a ransom for all (1 Timothy 2:5-6).

No one who comes to Christ for salvation will be turned away because Christ cannot save him. The apostle Paul says clearly, *"For by grace you have been saved through faith. And this is not your own doing; it is the gift of God, not a result of works, so that no one may boast"* Ephesians 2:8-9. Christ has already paid the price for our salvation. What is required of us then is to look to Jesus, trust Him and believe He has suffered the punishment for our sins. *"Whoever believes in him is not condemned, but whoever does not believe is condemned already, because he has not believed in the name of the only Son of God"* (John 3:18).

An invitation is given to all

The Lord Jesus Christ instructed His disciples to go into all the world and preach the gospel. This gospel message was to be presented to everyone. They were never told not to preach to certain individuals or nations. As the apostles preached, people believed and the Lord saved them.

The Bible says that *"God our Saviour, ...desires all people to be saved and to come to the knowledge of the truth"* (1 Timothy 2:3-4). In harmony with His nature God acted to save man from the result of his own deliberate sin and rebellion. The apostle Paul wrote, *"For the grace of God has appeared, bringing salvation for all people"* (Titus 2:11). The word 'grace' means undeserved mercy.

Whoever believes in Jesus will have eternal life (John 3:16). To use the words of Bishop J.C. Ryle, "the Bible always addresses men as free agents, accountable to God. Throughout Scripture it is a leading principle that man can lose his soul and that if he is lost, it will be by his own fault."

The commentator Robert McClurkin wrote, "no soul in hell will ever be able to say that God never loved him, that Christ never died for him, that the Spirit never strove with him." Even those in lands where the gospel was never preached have been made aware of God through creation and their conscience – God warns even the unreligious and leaves them to choose the right from the wrong.

Jesus said, "*I am the bread of life; whoever comes to me shall not hunger, and whoever believes in me shall never thirst... All that the Father gives me will come to me, and whoever comes to me I WILL never cast out*" (John 6:35, 37). "*This is the will of my Father, that everyone who looks on the Son and believes in him should have eternal life, and I will raise him up on the last day*" (John 6:40).

The Bible ends with this open invitation, "*The Spirit and the Bride say, "Come." And let the one who hears say, "Come." And let the one who is thirsty come; let the one who desires take the water of life without price*" (Revelation 22:17). The Bible invites every sinner to come to Jesus just as you are and know that He WILL welcome you.

Jesus said, "*This is the WILL of my Father, that everyone who looks on the Son and believes in him should have eternal life*" (John 6:40).

Questions for Reflection

1. Do we really need salvation?

2. Can we get to heaven without involving Jesus Christ?

3. If God is a God of love, surely everyone will get to heaven!

4. What does it mean to be 'born again'?

5. What does it mean, "whoever believes in Jesus Christ will have eternal life"?

6

"I Will" Make You Fishers of Men

Jesus said to His disciples,
"Follow me, and I will make you become fishers of men."
(Mark 1:16-20; Matthew 4:19-22)

When Jesus heard that John the Baptist had been put in prison He returned to Galilee and started to preach. As He walked beside the Sea of Galilee, He saw Simon and his brother Andrew casting a net into the lake, for they were fishermen. He said to them, *"Come, follow me, and I will make you fishers of men."* They immediately left their nets and followed Him. Later He saw two other brothers James and John in a boat preparing their nets and He called them also.

When Jesus called these men He was not inviting them to join an armed insurrection as they might have expected from the Messiah. He was calling them to something entirely different. Jesus called these fishermen at the beginning of His earthly ministry and then at the end, after His death and resurrection, He said to His disciples, *"Go into all the world and proclaim the gospel to the whole creation."*

The Call to follow Christ

The first part of their call was to follow Christ. This call was to fellowship and responsibility and to communicate with Christ. Before anyone can be used by Christ to become a fisher of men they must be with Christ, learn from Him and constantly depend upon Him.

These fishermen were called to follow a new Master. If someone wanted to learn from a rabbi, they chose their preferred teacher, followed him and eventually become his disciple. But here Jesus, as He frequently does during His lifetime, breaks the mould and doesn't follow the traditional way of doing things. That is always how Jesus works in reference to our lives - the initiative is His, not ours, as He seeks us out, and calls us to Himself. Later He tells His disciples, *"You did not choose me, but I chose you and appointed you that you should go and bear fruit"* (John 15:16).

When the rabbis made disciples, they taught them to follow the Torah - the Law of Moses. They were to follow the Law and the traditions of the elders, but it was different for Jesus' disciples. They were not to follow a code or a tradition passed on from past generations or the sayings of the Fathers, the teachings of the rabbis, the Law or Moses, but Jesus said, "Follow Me".

This call to the fishermen was simple, *"Follow me, and I will make you become fishers of men."* Yet, it was a call that changed their lives forever! For Jesus took these simple Galilean fishermen and transformed them into some of the greatest *"**fishers of men**"* the world has ever seen! These are challenging words for every reader today because Jesus wants to do in our lives just what He did in the lives of these men. He wants to take us, just as we are with all our faults, failures and rough edges and He wants to transform us into fishers of men and women.

These men left everything to follow Jesus. The word *"followed"* (Mark 1:18), means *"to cleave to another, conforming to*

His example". In other words, these men left their nets, their boats and life as they knew it, to cleave to Jesus and learn from Him. If we are going to become *"Fishers of Men"*, then we too must follow Jesus in this way.

When Jesus called the fishermen, they *"Immediately left their nets and followed him"* (Matthew 4:20). They left their job security, the only living they had known, to go with Jesus and follow Him. Later it is recorded in the Gospel of Matthew, *"As Jesus passed on from there, he saw a man called Matthew sitting at the tax booth, and he said to him, 'Follow me'"* (Matthew 9:9). Being a tax collector for the Romans was usually a very lucrative position but Matthew didn't think about all he was going to lose or leave behind. We are told, *"And he rose and followed him."* That is what it means to follow Christ. It is a radical change of lifestyle where we seek the kingdom above all things (Matthew 6:33). Jesus said to those who may suffer for following Christ, *"Do not fear those who kill the body but cannot kill the soul. Rather fear him who can destroy both soul and body in hell"* (Matthew 10:28).

Those who follow Christ must count the cost. Jesus said, *"Which of you, desiring to build a tower, does not first sit down and count the cost, whether he has enough to complete it"*? (Luke 14:28). Those who follow Christ are promised one day to enter the kingdom of heaven. This inheritance is not for this world or anything in this world, but for the world to come. God has prepared a kingdom for those who have repented of their sin and put their trust in Jesus as Saviour. If we have counted the cost and forsaken all others to follow Christ the promised inheritance is beyond our understanding.

The Call to become fishers of men

Jesus asks these fishermen to follow Him and He will make them fishers of men. He will teach them how to catch men. They watch Him as He speaks to the rich young ruler, and listen to His conversation with the woman at the well. They see Him dealing with Nicodemus when Jesus tells him he must be born again and they listen to His preaching in the Temple and also speaking to Zacchaeus. By the end of His ministry they will be equipped to go out and be fishers of men. What a tremendous challenge for these men! No longer will they be labouring and searching for fish but for men and women to win them for Christ.

Not only was this invitation to follow Christ and all that that involves but there is also an invitation to start a new mission. When Jesus said, *"I will make you become fishers of men"* He was obviously taking advantage of the profession of these brothers. They were fishermen, and so He is using that image, saying, 'If you will follow Me, I'm going to set you apart so that you will become My disciples to make My name known to the ends of the earth. You will be fishers of men.'

The image of the fisherman is used in the Old Testament by Jeremiah (16:16) but on that occasion the Lord will send for many fishermen and hunters to find people seeking to hide from the punishment of God. But when Jesus uses that image, He applies it to the mission of His disciples, the note of threat is missing. It is used in a positive and encouraging way. *"I will make you fishers of men."*

He doesn't say, 'Follow me and I will become your teacher.' His first words are about evangelism. You remember that the very last words Jesus spoke to these four fishermen were on the same theme. On the Mount of Ascension he said to them, *"You shall be my witnesses."* Here is an obligation that rests not upon the apostles alone, or on a chosen talented few, but upon every Christian. Every one whose life God's grace has touched has been called upon to be a witness for Christ in this world.

An old preacher said, "If a man has a soul, and he has, and if that soul can be won or lost for eternity, and it can, then the most important thing in the world is to bring a man to Jesus Christ." Do we really believe he was right? If so, we should gladly be a witness for Jesus and tell everyone of their need to be saved from the punishment of sin.

We do not automatically have a concern for evangelism. We do not drift into it, for it is a costly business. It cost God His Son. It cost Jesus death and sufferings on the cross. The problem we face is that so many people doubt that Jesus is the **only** Saviour of the world. They really don't believe that people need to believe in Him and have a personal relationship with Jesus Christ.

The Command to go and be fishers of men

Jesus calls His disciples not only to come to Him, but also to go for Him. Our mission is so important that Jesus repeated it five times in five different ways in five different books of the Bible, showing how important He considered this task. (Matthew 28:19; Mark 16:15; Luke 9:2; John 15: 5, 16; Acts 1:8).

Jesus said, *"Go therefore and make disciples of all nations, baptizing them in the name of the Father and of the Son and of the Holy Spirit"* (Matthew 28:19). The mission that Jesus had while on earth is now our mission since we are the Body of Christ. God wants to redeem human beings from Satan and reconcile them to Himself. Once we have committed our lives to Christ, He uses us to reach others; He saves us and then sends us out.

Jesus prays to his Father saying, *"As you sent me into the world, so I have sent them into the world"* (John 17:18). Therefore, when we become Christians we are sent as representatives of the one born in Bethlehem and crucified at Calvary. We are sent to announce that *the Father sent the Son.* We are sent to say and show that Jesus came into the world to save sinners (1 Timothy 1:15). What we proclaim is not ourselves, but Jesus and the good news about Him (2 Corinthians 4:5). We are not the message, but messengers of the message.

It is astonishing that God holds us responsible for the unbelievers that live around us. The Bible says, *"I have made you a watchman... whenever you hear a word from my mouth, you shall give them warning from me. ...if you give him no warning, nor speak to warn the wicked from his wicked way, ...his blood I will require at your hand..."* (Ezekiel 3:17-19). What a powerful challenge to every Christian. You may be the only Christian some people will ever know and your mission is to share Jesus with them.

To serve the Lord faithfully is not an easy task as we often face opposition and criticism. Some people may get excited and full of enthusiasm at first about witnessing and serving the Lord but are unable to keep it up. They cannot cope with the criticism (which will surely come). Others expect instant results and when it doesn't happen, they get discouraged and abandon the work. God has called each one of us to a lifetime campaign against a powerful enemy.

Although it is a great responsibility, it is also a tremendous honour to be used by God. Paul indicated that God has given us the privilege of urging everyone to come into His favour and be reconciled to Him.

The mission of Christ which is entrusted to the Church is still very far from completion. Jesus was sent to proclaim the Good News to all mankind. He preached the Good News through His words and actions. He appointed His followers to continue spreading the gospel message throughout the world.

The preparation to become a fisher of men

How does Jesus make us fishers of men? We could ask another question. How did Simon and Andrew, James and John become fishermen of fish? The answer, of course, is through watching their fathers over a long time, being with them and helping them on the boats. Their fathers showed them all that was involved in the work of a fisherman.

When the Lord Jesus appointed His twelve disciples to the ministry of soul winning *"...he appointed twelve (whom he also named apostles) so that they might be with him and he might send them out to preach"* (Mark 3:14). He did not send them out at once - for about three years the Master trained His men, by instruction, by discipline and by example, in order that He might send them forth to be witnesses for Him to the far ends of the earth. Only by being with the Lord Jesus shall we come to know what is involved.

So we learn from watching how Christ called men and women and from following the example of His disciples. Jesus sets us an example on:

1. *'personal evangelism'* - thirty-five personal interviews of Jesus alone are recorded in the Gospel.

2. *'spontaneous evangelism'* - Jesus at the well (John 4:1-26), Peter and John at the gate Beautiful (John 3:1-12).

3. *'dialogue evangelism'* - Paul at Mars' Hill (Acts 17:21-34) and Apollos at Ephesus (Acts 18:24-28).

4. *'systematic evangelism'* - the seventy-two sent out by Jesus two by two (Luke 10:1-12), the house-to-house visitation (Acts 5:42).

5. *'literary evangelism'* - Luke 1:1-4 and John 20:31, both clearly state the evangelistic intent of the writers of these Gospels.

During Jesus' earthly ministry, the disciples did everything with Him - they walked, talked and ate with Him. They not only listened to His words, but they observed and imitated the Living Word. This (and the Holy Spirit) prepared them to take the gospel to the ends of the earth.

We cannot expect any one method to work with everyone and God may use a combination of many different approaches to win any individual.

Jesus told His disciples that they would become more successful "fishers of men" than He had been. Paul records what happened after the death and resurrection of Christ, *"Then he appeared to more than five hundred brothers at one time"* (1 Corinthians 15:6), but Peter in his first sermon reached thousands. There are many people recorded by Luke in the book of Acts who believed. *"Many of those who had heard the word believed, and the number of the men came to about five thousand"* (Acts 4:4).

Men and women must be brought face to face with the risen Christ, this is a priority. Lost sinners must be brought to the place of true repentance towards God and faith in our Lord Jesus Christ. Every Christian ought to be able to bear faithful witness to the Saviour. Therefore, we should go into all the world with Christ's presence, *"Behold, I am with you always, to the end of the age"* (Matthew 28:20).

Essential preparation to become "fishers of men" is to believe that the Reformed Faith, as we confess it, is both true and important. The message of the Gospel involves the truth of the virgin birth, life, death, resurrection and ascension of Jesus Christ the Son of God. While some Christians are called to be pastors or evangelists (Ephesians 4:11), all are expected to be witnesses and tell the lost about the Saviour. It must be made known that Jesus said, *"I am the way, and the truth, and the life. No one comes to the Father except through me"* (John 14:6).

What is required to be a successful witness?

We would all acknowledge that there would be great difficulty for a Christian to go to a child in one of the largest slums in Asia, where it is home to more than a million people and say to him, "Trust in Jesus", because he has no idea who Jesus is. Similarly to say to a boy standing on the corner of a street in London, England, to trust in Jesus he has little idea of the identity of 'Jesus Christ', except to use His name as a swear word. We first have to tell people about the person and work of Jesus Christ.

In the 18th century when John Wesley and George Whitefield lived, large numbers of people would gather to hear them preach. In those days there was some knowledge of the Bible but we don't live in such favoured times today. We are living at a time when second and third generations have had no church connection. People have not heard of the saving work of Christ. *"How can they believe in the one of whom they have not heard?"* (Romans 10:14).

Therefore, before we appeal to people to make a decision to accept Christ's offer of salvation, they must be given knowledge of who Jesus is, and why he is worthy of their trust. Perhaps as you read this book you have come to realise that you are also lacking in basic knowledge as to who Jesus is. When Jesus was witnessing to Nicodemus He said, *"We speak what we know"* (John 3:11). Many people are looking for those who can speak with conviction and authority about their faith in the Lord Jesus Christ. To be a faithful witness we need to possess the unshakable assurance that we know in whom we have believed.

On the other hand perhaps you know about Jesus, but as yet He is not your Saviour, and you have neglected to take any action about personal faith in Christ; as a result your condemnation is greater because you are neglecting His offer of mercy. *"How shall we escape if we neglect such a great salvation?"* (Hebrews 2:3). It is sad to think that many people pass into a lost eternity and are separated from Christ for all eternity because during their lifetime they neglected their salvation. If Satan can persuade you to neglect your salvation he is well pleased. However, God's offer of mercy is open for you today - believe in the Lord Jesus Christ and you will be saved.

The gospel message has the power to change and rescue lives from a lost eternity. There is power in no other message. Paul said, *"For I am not ashamed of the gospel, for it is the power of God for salvation to everyone who believes, to the Jew first and also to the Greek"* (Romans 1:16).

It must be recognised that no rigid rule is laid down for personal soul-winning. God is sovereign in His work and never deals with two people in exactly the same way. A true fisherman knows that in order to catch fish, you have to use the right bait. We must offer the only effective net - the gospel of Jesus Christ. *"For the word of the cross is folly to those who are perishing, but to us who are being saved it is the power of God"* (1 Corinthians 1:18). This was Jesus' message to Peter and Andrew - follow Me, learn of Me, know and understand My mission and My message. Only then will you be able to be "fishers of men".

The faithful fisherman receives his rewards

When the fisherman uses the right bait and goes to the right place to fish he will come home rejoicing with his catch of fish to share with his family and friends. Similarly the one who obeys God's command to be a "fisher of men" will also receive his reward. Paul said, *"He who plants and he who waters are one, and each will receive his wages according to his labour"* (1 Corinthians 3:8). We are God's fellow workers.

The purpose and work of fishermen is to catch fish. This is also the work to which Christians have been called, to bring souls to God. Fishermen work hard and are exposed to the cold and wet, so is the work of evangelism. The Christian must be willing to persevere in spite of difficulties. Fishermen identify the places where they should cast their nets, and where they may expect fish. Therefore Christians should pay attention to the places where they can witness for Christ - in private conversation or in the public gathering of people.

Fishermen may toil all night and catch nothing but they don't give up fishing. Christians may witness and labour for years and "catch" few souls but that does not mean they give up. Jesus may come along unexpectedly and ask us to *"Cast the net on the right side of the boat, and you will find some..."* (John 21:6), an act that seemed to make no sense, but which brought a great catch. As Christians walk closely with God, they may sense His Spirit telling them to talk to someone about Him, or do something unusual which God may use to bring someone to come to know Him.

God tells us in His Word, *"He who wins souls is wise"* (Proverbs 11:30). Everything we do to help win souls for the Kingdom of God will receive rewards. In 1 Corinthians 3, Paul teaches that every Christian's life is like a building. For a building to be strong and to remain it needs a good foundation, therefore a Christian's life must be built upon a strong foundation which is Jesus Christ (1 Corinthians 3:11).

It is our responsibility to be careful how we build! *"If anyone builds on the foundation with gold, silver, precious stones, wood, hay, or straw, each builder's work will be plainly seen,"* (1 Corinthians 3:12). These materials and the building represent our faith and character structure. Each Christian's work will be examined, that which is permanent - gold, silver and precious stones - will receive a reward. That which is temporary - wood, hay and stubble - will be burned and destroyed (1 Corinthians 3:13). This does not refer to salvation. It refers to the rewards that some saved people will receive and that others will not.

If our efforts are not built upon true biblical principles combined with a strong commitment, we are building with the symbolical... wood, hay, straw mentioned in 1 Corinthians 3:12. Our faith structure will collapse under trials just as a building made of wood will quickly burn to ashes if overtaken by fire.

A young man came to Jesus and asked what he must do to get eternal life. Jesus talked to him about obeying the commandments and then said, *"come, follow me"* (Matthew 19:16-22). However, unlike the two sets of brothers (Peter and Andrew; James and John) who immediately followed Jesus as recorded in Mark 1:16-20; Matthew 4:19-22, we are told he refused to do that, *"because he had great wealth."* He obviously considered following Jesus was too costly; it was too much for him. He was unaware of the fact that the cost in following Jesus may be great but the gain is always infinitely greater.

People matter to God and ought to matter to every Christian. The daily routine can suddenly change when the unexpected opportunity comes to be a witness for Christ. It is amazing to realise that what we do each day has meaning in God's plan and purpose of events. The personal benefits are great to those who are prepared to be a witness for Christ and be a "fisher of men". We should not forget *"there is joy before the angels of God over one sinner who repents"* (Luke 15:10).

There is a cost for following Jesus, but there are great rewards in fellowship with Christ. Some people may think they may become rich without Christ but true riches can only be found in Christ. It is a tragedy if someone says 'no' to Jesus because they think there is something more urgent or more rewarding by going another way. Jesus is inviting you to leave whatever you are holding on to and follow Him. Do not delay. Jesus says, *"Follow me, and I will make you become fishers of men."*

Questions for Reflection

1. Before a Christian becomes a 'fisher of men' is it important to receive a call?

2. Do you think it is necessary to receive training/preparation about witnessing for Christ?

3. Should only some Christians be witnesses for Christ?

4. What different methods have you used to witness for Christ?

5. Do you think the rewards justify the 'cost' of being a 'fisherman' for Christ?

7
"I Will" Build My Church

Jesus said to Peter, *"You are Peter, and on this rock I will
build my church, and the gates of hell shall not prevail against it."*
(Matthew 16:18)

When people are asked what church they attend they usually
refer to a certain building. Others refer to the church as an
organization - the Roman Catholic Church, the Anglican Church,
the Presbyterian Church, the Baptist Church among many others.

The early Christian Church had no buildings, at least not in
the sense of what we would consider church buildings today. First
century Christians were often persecuted and as a result met in
secret, usually in homes. As the influence of Christianity spread,
eventually buildings dedicated to worship were established and
became what we know today as churches. In this sense, then, the
church consists of people not buildings. Fellowship, worship and
ministry are all conducted by people, not buildings.

What is the Church?

Jesus was the first person to mention the church. Jesus asked
His disciples, *"Who do people say that I am?"* (Mark 8:27). The
disciples told Him what people were saying about Him; that He

was John the Baptist, Elijah, Jeremiah, or one of the old prophets back from the dead. But Jesus wanted the personal opinions of the disciples saying, *"But who do you say that I am?"* (Matthew 16:15).

Without hesitation, Peter replied, *"You are the Christ, the Son of the living God"* (Matthew 16:16). Jesus answered him, *"Blessed are you, Simon Bar-Jonah! For flesh and blood has not revealed this to you, but my Father who is in heaven. And I tell you, you are Peter, and on this rock I will build my church, and the gates of hell shall not prevail against it"* (Matthew 16:17-18).

This was not the first time a similar confession had been made: when Jesus revealed to Nathanael that He had seen him under the fig tree before Philip found him, Nathanael declared, *"Rabbi, you are the Son of God! You are the King of Israel!"* (John 1:49). Also, when Jesus walked on the water to be with His disciples who were in a boat during a storm, Peter declared, *"Truly you are the Son of God"* (Matthew14:33).

When Andrew brought his brother Simon to Jesus it was because of his conviction as to who Jesus was, *"We have found the Messiah"* (John 1:41). Peter gave a confession of faith at a time when the crowds left Jesus after His sermon on the Bread of Life, *"Lord, to whom shall we go? You have the words of eternal life, and we have believed, and have come to know, that you are the Holy One of God"* (John 6:68-69).

However, this confession of Peter was different from the others. It was not through human intellect or merit that Peter confessed Christ to be the Messiah. After all, *"no one can say "Jesus is Lord" except in the Holy Spirit"* (1 Corinthians 12:3). Only God can reveal His Son to the human mind. Jesus said, *"no one knows the Son except the Father, and no one knows the Father except the Son and anyone to whom the Son chooses to reveal him"* (Matthew 11:27). It is only by divine revelation we can know Christ.

The meaning of 'Rock' in Scripture

At this point in Matthew's Gospel, Jesus gave Simon the name Peter. "*I tell you, you are Peter, and on this rock I will build my church, and the gates of hell shall not prevail against it*" (Matthew16:18). Matthew wrote his Gospel for a Jewish audience. He expected his readers to be familiar with Old Testament imagery.

Peter was a Jew and with his knowledge of the Old Testament would know that '*Rock*' throughout the Hebrew Scripture is never used symbolically of man, but always of God. In the Old Testament God is referred to as a Rock: "*Ascribe greatness to our God! The Rock, his work is perfect, for all his ways are justice*" (Deuteronomy 32:3-4).

In the Psalms, David continually wrote of the Rock, not as if it represented a man, but clearly as a representation of God. "*The LORD is my rock and my fortress and my deliverer, my God, my rock, in whom I take refuge*" (Psalm 18:2); "*For who is God, but the LORD? And who is a rock, except our God?*" (Psalm 18:31). David makes it clear that '*God alone*' is the true Rock in whom we should put our trust for salvation, "*He alone is my rock and my salvation*" (Psalm 62:2).

Throughout the Bible, the concept of "the Rock" has always referred to God and to Christ. Paul clearly defined the "Rock" that gave water to the children of Israel in the days of Moses: "*They drank from the spiritual Rock that followed them, and the Rock was Christ*" (1 Corinthians 10:4).

Did Jesus say the Church would be built on Peter?

Peter is from *petros*, a masculine form of the Greek word for small stone, whereas rock is from *petra*, a different form of the same basic word, referring to a rocky mountain or peak. What Jesus said to Peter could be translated, 'you are *stone* and upon this *bedrock* I will build My church.' His choice of words would indicate that the rock on which the church would be built was something other than Peter.

When using *Petros* as "a movable stone," Jesus is using a word with a double meaning. Jesus said to Simon, *"you are Petros (a movable stone), and on this Petra (a large unmovable rock) I will build my ekklesia (Assembly)"* (Matthew16:18). The meaning is that Petros is just one stone in an assembly of stones. The assembly is built on the immovable Rock that is Jesus.

Although many believe Jesus noted the meaning of Peter's name here as *rock*, there was no supremacy given to him by Christ. Rather, Jesus was referring to Peter's declaration: *"You are the Christ, the Son of the living God."* This confession of faith is *'the rock'* upon which the church is built, and just like Peter, everyone who confesses Jesus Christ as Lord is a part of the church.

This was the understanding of the early Christians, and there is no record either in the Bible or in early church history that Peter was considered the "infallible" head of the Christian church. Yet, the question remains: Why did Jesus say what He did to Peter?

If Jesus appointed Peter as the head of the church, why did the other disciples quarrel among themselves as to who would be the greatest? (Luke 9:46). If this decision had already been made by Christ, why should the others be anxious about it? The other disciples would have submitted to the wish of their Master. Therefore, it seems clear that no such appointment had been made by Jesus.

If Peter is the rock on which Christ was to build His church, Peter could not be overcome and the gates of hell could not prevail against him. But the fact is that he was overcome, and the gates of hell did prevail against him. Didn't he deny his Lord? This was after Christ told him that the Rock was not to be overcome. Jesus told Peter on one occasion: *"Get behind me, Satan! You are a hindrance to me. For you are not setting your mind on the things of God, but on the things of man"* (Matthew 16:23).

For centuries, there have been those who have maintained that Jesus Christ founded His church upon the Apostle Peter, and that the office and jurisdiction of the bishop of Rome represents an "unbroken" line of apostolic succession from Peter to the present day. There are those who interpret Jesus as saying, "You are Peter, and upon you, Peter, I will build My church." However, as we have seen Peter could not be the rock on which Christ would build His church.

According to Roman Catholic tradition the Church considers its bishops to be the successors of Jesus' apostles and the Church's leader, the Bishop of Rome (also known as the Pope), to be the sole successor to St. Peter who ministered in Rome in the first century AD, after his appointment by Jesus as head of the church.

Attempts were made to reform (change and improve) the Catholic Church when a German monk called Martin Luther protested about the teaching and practices within the Catholic Church. This led to the Reformation which began in 1517 and the development of Protestant Churches in Western Europe.

Many people and governments adopted the Protestant teaching of Scripture, while others remained faithful to the Catholic Church. This led to a split in the Church. This movement known as the 'Reformation' claims to be faithful to Scripture and believes that Jesus Christ is the 'Head of the Church' and not Peter.

Who was the Church built on?

Jesus said that the rock He would build His church on was not the masculine *"petros"* but the feminine *"petra."* What, then, is the true significance of our Lord's word about building His Church on a 'Rock'? The two Greek words used indicate the Lord was talking about two distinct things. His choice of words would show that the rock on which the church would be built was something other than Peter. 'This rock' that the church is built on is not Peter, but the confession Peter made, *"You are the Christ, the Son of the living*

God." Jesus replied, *"Blessed are you, Simon Bar-Jonah! For flesh and blood has not revealed this to you, but my Father who is in heaven"* (Matthew 16:16-17).

Interpreting Christ as the rock upon which the church would be built also agrees with other statements in Scripture. Paul warned, *"For no one can lay a foundation other than that which is laid, which is Jesus Christ"* (1 Corinthians 3:11). Here, he emphasizes that Christ is the foundation upon which the church is built. In Ephesians, Paul speaks of the church as having been *"built on the foundation of the apostles and prophets, Christ Jesus himself being the cornerstone"* (Ephesians 2:20). Here Paul pictures Christ as the *'corner stone'* and the apostles and prophets as secondary stones.

Neither Peter nor any of his successors were the head of the true church. There is no man on earth who is the head of the Church. The Lord Jesus Christ and He alone, is the head of His body which is the Church. He says that there is no remedy for sin, and there is no salvation, except through faith in the Lord Jesus Christ. God the Father sent Jesus into the world, as Peter said, *"He himself bore our sins in his body on the tree"* (1 Peter 2:24).

Paul explains this when he says, *"The head of every man is Christ"* (1 Corinthians 11:3). God *"put all things under his feet and gave him as head over all things to the church, which is his body"* (Ephesians 1:22). As we look at the context, this explains that Jesus is the head of every person and also of the church. We are responsible to the head, which is Christ, and not to men who try to mislead the work of Christ and take His place.

The context of Matthew 16:13-20 is not about Peter; it is about Jesus. It starts with a question that Jesus raised about His identity: *"Who do people say that the Son of Man is?"* (Matthew 16:13). It reached a climax with Peter's declaration: *"You are the Christ, the Son of the living God"* (Matthew 16:16). It concludes with the Lord warning His disciples *"to tell no one that he was the Christ"* (Matthew 16:20).

The word "church" as rendered in the New Testament comes from the Greek term 'ekklesia' which is formed from two Greek words meaning "an assembly" and "to call out" or "called out ones." This means the New Testament church is a body of believers who have been called out from the world by God to live as His people under the authority of Jesus Christ.

There are many instances in Scripture where Jesus is referred to as the head of the church, and the church is referred to as the 'body of Christ.' *"Now you are the body of Christ, and each one of you is a part of it"* (1 Corinthians 12:27). We also read that Jesus is *"the head of the body, the church. He is the beginning, the firstborn from the dead, that in everything he might be preeminent"* (Colossians 1:18).

The New Testament has many names for the church: it is spoken of as God's building, His planting, His vineyard, His temple, His household, His olive tree, His city, and His people. But with all these illustrations, God does not see different 'churches' or denominations, He sees those who have accepted the good news of the gospel, and who live by faith in Him. God primarily identifies those who belong to His church according to the love that they show toward others: *"By this all people will know that you are my disciples, if you have love for one another"* (John 13:35).

Before His ascension, Jesus' final instructions to His disciples were: *"All authority in heaven and on earth has been given to me. Go therefore and make disciples of all nations, baptizing them in the name of the Father and of the Son and of the Holy Spirit, teaching them to observe all that I have commanded you. I am with you always, to the end of the age"* (Matthew 28:18-20). He also reminded them, *"You will receive power when the Holy Spirit has come upon you, and you will be my witnesses in Jerusalem and in all Judea and Samaria, and to the end of the earth"* (Acts 1:8).

In Bible terms, the church is made up of every person who has a personal relationship with Jesus Christ - all those who have received salvation through faith in Him.

The Church is the Bride of Christ

The *ekklēsia* is not directly called "the bride of Christ" in the New Testament. However, the apostle Paul describes the relationship of Christ and *ekklēsia* to be like that of husband and wife. *"Husbands, love your wives, as Christ loved the church and gave himself up for her"* (Ephesians 5:25).

When John the Baptist was asked if he were the Christ his reply was *"I am not the Christ, but I have been sent before him."* John then compared Jesus to the bridegroom and himself to the friend or witness, *"The one who has the bride is the bridegroom. The friend of the bridegroom, who stands and hears him, rejoices greatly at the bridegroom's voice. Therefore this joy of mine is now complete"* (John 3:29). At a marriage once the bridegroom and bride have been brought together the work of the witness (best man or friend) is finished. John rejoices at the bridegroom's voice (Jesus) and had claimed His bride (the church). Because a bridegroom must have a bride, this is the only place in the Gospels that the bride is mentioned, but, all other mentions of the bridegroom imply the bride.

When Jesus was asked why His disciples did not fast, but the followers of John and the Pharisees did, Jesus answered: *"Can the wedding guests fast while the bridegroom is with them?"* (Mark 2:19). Here Jesus is suggesting that He was the bridegroom, as John had called Him (John 3:29), and that His disciples were the children of the bride; and that it was very unsuitable for them, and very unreasonable to desire them to fast at such a time. Therefore the answer returned by Christ to the question is, *"as long as they* (the bride) *have the bridegroom* (Jesus) *with them, they cannot fast. The days will come when the bridegroom is taken away from them, and then they will fast in that day."* (Mark 2:19b-20).

Believers in Jesus Christ are the bride of Christ, and we wait with great anticipation for the day when we will be united with our

Bridegroom. Until then, we remain faithful to Him and say with all the redeemed of the Lord, *"Come, Lord Jesus!"* (Revelation 22:20). The church is comprised of those who have trusted in Jesus Christ as their personal Saviour and have received eternal life. Christ, the Bridegroom, has sacrificially and lovingly chosen the church to be His bride (Ephesians 5:25-27).

The symbolism of marriage is applied to Christ and the body of believers known as the church. Just as there was a betrothal period in biblical times during which the bride and groom were separated until the wedding, so is the bride of Christ separate from her Bridegroom during the church age. Her responsibility during the betrothal period is to be faithful to Him (2 Corinthians 11:2; Ephesians 5:24). This is also implied in John 14:1-3 when Jesus talked about making a place at His Father's house for us. This is similar to when a man proposes to a woman and they are engaged. The man goes away and prepares a house and home for his new bride. When the work is done and everything is ready, he comes to call for his bride.

The image of bridegroom would have been significant to the Jewish people, for Jehovah had a "marriage covenant" with the nation (Isaiah 54:5; Jeremiah 2:2; Ezekiel 16:3). However, as it is recorded many times, Israel had been unfaithful to her vows and God had to punish her. Today God is calling out a people for His name, the church, the bride of Christ. One day the Bridegroom will come to claim His bride and take her home to heaven. Will you be ready when the Bridegroom returns? (Matthew 25:1-13).

The Visible and Invisible Church

Where two or three are gathered together for fellowship in the name of Christ you have a visible Church. There will always be the believer and unbeliever worshipping together until Christ returns. It is visible because it has outward characteristics which can be seen. These characteristics are the true preaching of the Word of

God, the right administration of the sacraments and the proper exercise of discipline. Every local congregation is a visible church.

The visible church exists in order to offer living worship to God. This is simply to give God His "worth-ship." Worship is something the people of God do together. The Church also exists in order to bear living witness to the world. It is literally a society for the proclamation of the gospel - an evangelistic society. The Church also exists as it follows God's plan. God has given gifts to various men and women in the Church in order that they can share in its overall ministry. Every Church member has a gift of some sort by which the body of Christ can be built up.

The invisible or true church comprises only those whose names have been written in the Lamb's Book of Life. What people see at a human level is a group of people whose names are on a communicants' roll. What God sees is those who have been converted to Jesus Christ and whose names are written in Heaven's roll. Has your name been written in the Lamb's Book of Life? If not, give serious consideration to the need to repent of your sin and trust Christ as your personal Saviour.

When speaking of the church, theologians often use the terms - the visible and local church as opposed to the invisible or universal church. The visible and local churches are what we see around us and around the world, as well as the members of those churches. The invisible or universal church, however, refers to all believers everywhere and is one church, united in Christ. Everyone in the universal church is a true believer.

The Church is said to be one holy, catholic apostolic church. It is 'one' because of the basic unity of the people of God. They share His divine nature and acknowledge one Lord, faith and baptism.

The Church is 'holy' because it has been set apart by God. The Church is 'catholic' or 'universal' because it is the world fellowship of believing people, including all believers of all ages in all lands.

The Church is 'apostolic', not because it can trace its history back to the Apostles through a succession of prelates who laid hands upon each other, but because it maintains the 'apostolic truth and mission' enshrined in the Apostles' doctrine and preaching.

Jesus builds the church and He is the Cornerstone. He is the sole head of the church. The promise of Christ is, *the gates of hell will not prevail against it.* How is it that the church triumphs over hell? Not because of any virtue of the church itself or her pastors or elders. It is because of the great Builder of the church. We are brought back to His question: *"who do you say that I am?"* - He is *"the Christ, the Son of the Living God."* If you make that confession, you stand on the one foundation. And if you are standing on Christ - the one foundation - then you become a 'living stone' and He has built you into His Church.

This is why no other institution is given this promise, not education, schools, government or even a para-church - a Christian faith-based organisation that works outside and across denominations. It is the church that is promised victory over hell. The church is Jesus' victory - it is the demonstration of the wisdom and power of God. There is no guarantee that any individual local church will be successful or last any length of time. But with great confidence, we know that the Church of Jesus Christ will bear fruit in every nation, tongue and tribe. We know this because Christ has pledged himself to this. So we go forward with great anticipation in His name.

Since the days when Adam and Eve were in the Garden of Eden, Satan has made every effort to destroy God's people. He has used many means to wipe the church off the map, but has been unsuccessful, because there is power available in the name of Jesus to build the church victorious and not listen to the lies of the adversary.

Jesus said, I will build 'my' Church

Jesus did not say "*You* will build *your* church." Nor did He say, "*I* will build *your* church." Jesus did not say, "*You* will build *my* church." What He actually said was, "*I* will build *my* church." He reserved for Himself this most important work. It is comforting to know that we are not responsible for the success of the church and that those who preach and serve Christ, are not responsible for saving people but are expected to be faithful in their witnessing.

Although Peter recognized himself as an apostle (1 Peter 1:1; 2 Peter 1:1), he never claimed a superior title, rank, or privilege over the other apostles. He even referred to himself as a "fellow elder" (1 Peter 5:1) and as "a servant" of Christ (2 Peter 1:1). Far from claiming honour and respect for himself, he warns his fellow elders to guard against domineering over those under their pastoral care (1 Peter 5:3). The only glory he claimed for himself was that which is shared by all believers and which is yet "*to be revealed... when the chief Shepherd appears*" (1 Peter 1,4).

"*I will build my church*" - The first word of the statement is "I". Who is this "I" who made this promise? This marks the unique position of Christ as Lord. Nobody else is in a position to say what follows this "I". It marks Christ's Lordship. Jesus is the only rightful founder and head of the church, not you or me or anyone else. It is the same "I" as in "*I am the way, the truth and the life*" (John 14:6). "*I am the good shepherd. The good shepherd lays down his life for the sheep*" (John 10:11). No one else can say that.

"*Will*" - When Jesus said "will", He expressed His authority (Matthew 28:18). His will is supreme except for the will of His Father. When Jesus says, "I will" we can be sure He will carry out what He has promised. We have already looked at some of the "I wills" of Jesus and are comforted by what He has said. "*I will give you rest*" (Matthew 11:28). "*I will not leave you as orphans*" (John 14:18). Therefore, we can be sure of what He has promised will come to pass.

"Build" - When Jesus said "build", He was stating the nature of His work. When the disciples urged Jesus to eat He said, *"I have food to eat that you do not know about ... My food is to do the will of him who sent me and to accomplish his work. My Father is working until now, and I am working"* (John 4:34, John 5:17). Seeking to promote a denomination is not the work of Christ. Building large church buildings or cathedrals is not the work of Christ. He is only interested in building 'His' Church - that is what He died for. Are we doing Christ's work - not building our own ego, legacy or building to leave behind for others to admire or praise, but are we labouring with the Master to build His Church?

"My" - When Jesus said *"my"*, He indicated to whom the church belongs. It marks Christ's possession. It was His blood that purchased the church. The only church worth belonging to is *"the church of God, which he obtained with his own blood"* (Acts 20:28). The church's one foundation is Jesus Christ her Lord. *"For no one can lay a foundation other than that which is laid, which is Jesus Christ"* (1 Corinthians 3:11). Christ is the chief corner stone, no one else. The church *"is built on the foundation of the apostles and prophets, Christ Jesus himself being the cornerstone"* (Ephesians 2:20). There is only one Cornerstone that is Christ. He is the sole head of the church. The church is His bride whom He loves. She belongs to no other. *"Christ loved the church and gave himself up for her"* (Ephesians 5:25-27).

"Church" - When Jesus said "church", He expresses His call to the world. Jesus calls everyone into His one true church - the "called out" people (*ekklesia*). The church is a body of believers who have been called out from the world by God to live as His people under the authority of Jesus Christ. God *"who saved us and called us to a holy calling, not because of our works but because of his own purpose and grace, which he gave us in Christ Jesus before the ages began"* (2 Timothy 1:9).

In every word of the statement *"I will build my church"* we are brought to the realization that Christ's church is what we should be restoring and establishing in the world. Let's work together in going back to the one true church of Christ. No other "church" will do. Jesus WILL build His church and the gates of hell shall not prevail against it.

Questions for Reflection

1.   How would you answer someone who claims that Peter was the foundation stone of the Church?

2.   Could you prove from Scripture that Christ is the Head of the Church?

3.   What does it mean that the Church is the 'Bride of Christ'?

4.   Are you a member of the 'Invisible Church'?

5.   Did Jesus say that we would build His Church?

8

"I Will" Raise Them Up at the Last Day

"God raised the Lord and WILL also raise us up by his power"
(1 Corinthians 6:14). *"This is the will of him who sent me,
that I shall lose none of all that he has given, but raise them up
at the last day."* (John 6:39)

The resurrection was central to the teaching and preaching
of the Apostles. Paul said, *"If Christ has not been raised, then
our preaching is in vain and your faith is in vain... And if
Christ has not been raised, your faith is futile and you are still
in your sins."* (1 Corinthians 15:14,17)

The resurrection of Jesus Christ is not just an interesting story; it is
an historical fact, based on eye witness accounts. To be a believer,
one must believe in the resurrection. If there was no resurrection,
then Jesus is still dead; He wasn't the Son of God and there is no
forgiveness of sins. It was through the resurrection that Christ
defeated death and the devil. Christ's resurrection guarantees the
resurrection of all believers. *"Christ is the firstfruits of those who
have fallen asleep"* (1 Corinthians 15:20-23), giving promise that
those who belong to Christ will also be raised in the last day.
Without the resurrection there is no Christianity.

Proof of the Resurrection of Christ

Frequently in the gospels Christ predicted both His death and resurrection (Matthew 16:21; 17:23; 26:32; Mark 9:30-32; Luke 9:22; Luke 18:31-34; John 2:19-22; John 10:17-18).

Christ made many appearances after His death to His disciples, to individuals and to groups of people: He appeared to Mary Magdalene (John 20:11-17); to a group of women (Matthew 28:9-10); to the apostle Peter (Luke 24:34); to His disciples on several occasions (John 20:19-23, 20:24-29); to seven disciples by the Sea of Galilee (John 21:1-14); to more than five hundred people (1 Corinthians 15:6), then to James and all the Apostles (1 Corinthians 15:7). He made at least seventeen appearances after His resurrection. The circumstances and number of witnesses all confirm that it really was Christ who made these appearances.

Many of these witnesses did not know what to believe at first and had to be convinced by the evidence that it was Jesus. The women and the disciples who went to the tomb were satisfied when they saw that it was empty; Thomas did not believe what the other disciples had told him, he had to see Jesus for himself. The disciples went back to fishing believing that the crucifixion and death of Jesus was the end of Jesus' ministry, but this changed when Jesus appeared to them on the sea shore.

Following these appearances the change in the attitude of the disciples was remarkable. After the crucifixion they were dejected, downhearted and sad, but after His resurrection they were filled with joy and went out to preach and proclaim that Christ had risen from the dead. Jesus appeared to His disciples and informed them that they would be filled with the Holy Spirit and then they were to go out and be witnesses for Him (Acts 1:8). Jesus is showing that the power of the church and witnessing comes from the Holy Spirit and not from man. Every Christian is encouraged to bear witness to their risen Saviour. The resurrection was proof that Jesus really was who He claimed to be - the Son of God and Saviour of the world. He died for our sins and rose again in victory. When Christ rose from the dead, He became the "firstfruits" of the dead (1 Corinthians 15:20).

The view that the body was stolen is unreasonable and absurd in view of the precautions taken by the authorities when His body was placed in the tomb (Matthew 27:62-66); also the Jews were unable to produce the body of Christ to prove that He had not risen. The survival and growth of the church and its impact on the world's civilization proved that Christ must have risen from the dead.

The Purpose of the Resurrection of Christ

In 1 Corinthians 15:12-19 Paul shows that everything stands or falls with Christ's bodily resurrection. If Christ had not risen, preaching is useless (v.14), the Corinthian's were yet in their sins (v.17), those who have fallen asleep in Christ are lost (v.18), and Christians are of all people most to be pitied (v.19).

The book of Acts emphasises that the apostolic preaching was based on the resurrection of Christ (Acts 2:24, 32; 3:15, 26; 4:10; 10:40; 13:30-37). This can also be noted by Paul (Romans 4:24ff. 6:4, 9; 7:4; 8:11; 10:9; 1 Corinthians 6:14; 15:4; Galatians 1:1 Colossians 2:12; 2 Timothy 2:8) and also Peter (1 Peter 1:21; 3:21). The resurrection is clearly an essential part of the gospel.

Paul states that if Christ was not raised, then those who have died are lost forever; our hope would only be for this life, which would make no sense at all. However, since Scripture is clear that Christ was raised from the dead, then those who have died in Christ are not lost. Also we have hope in Jesus Christ for eternal life in the age to come. Our hope beyond death is based on the remarkable fact of the resurrection of Jesus Christ.

The resurrection of Christ is the most important proof for the deity of Jesus Christ. Jesus, as the Good Shepherd, voluntarily and willingly gave up His life, but three days later He took up His life again and rose from the dead, the Father gave Him this authority (John 10:17-18). In some places in Scripture we are told that it was the Father who raised the Son (Acts 2:32; Romans 6:4; Hebrews 13:20). In John 5:17, 19 we are told that the Son had authority to take up His own life again. There is no contradiction here as the Father and the Son worked together in perfect harmony. Previous to this Jesus had hinted that He had power to raise Himself from the dead (John 5:26).

Paul affirms that the resurrection of Christ proves *"what is the immeasurable greatness of his power towards us who believe"* (Ephesians 1:19-21), and gives victory over sin and death. The resurrection is therefore the cornerstone of our Christian faith. Because Christ is raised, our Christian faith is sure, the ultimate victory of Christ is certain, and our Christian faith is completely justified.

The resurrection was a work of the Triune God. The Bible teaches the resurrection of the body (1 Corinthians 15:20, 23; Colossians 1:18; Revelation 1:5). This implies that the people of God will be like their heavenly Lord. Paul says that Jesus was *"raised for our justification"* (Romans 4:25). When God raised Jesus from the dead, He was affirming Jesus' sacrifice on our behalf was accepted. He was demonstrating His approval of Jesus' suffering and dying for our sins, the penalty for sin was paid. Jesus had to rise from the dead to prove His work was complete; salvation and forgiveness of sins are now proclaimed in the name of Jesus. As Hebrews 1:3 tells us, *"After making purification for sins, He sat down at the right hand of the Majesty on high."* Jesus sat down at God's right hand because His work was completed.

The resurrection of Christ has an important part in the application of salvation. God raised Him up and exalted Him to His right hand that He might be the head over all things to the church (Ephesians 1:20-22). It was necessary for Him to rise before the Holy Spirit, the third person of the Trinity, could descend upon the early church and baptise the believers (John 1:33; Acts 1:5; 2:32ff.; 11:15-17; 1 Corinthians 12:13). His death, resurrection and ascension are preparatory to His bestowing gifts on the believer (Ephesians 4:7-13).

The nature of Christ's Resurrected body

There have been those who have promoted the theory that Jesus did not actually die, but that he fainted or fell into a swoon, from which He recovered after being placed in the cool air of the tomb. Joseph of Arimathea and Nicodemus had used spices when they wrapped His body before burial and these had also contributed towards His recovery. This, however, is contrary to the evidence presented in the Scriptures. That Christ actually died, is evident from the fact that the centurion and the soldiers declared Him to be dead (Mark 15:45; John 19:33); the women came with the expectation of anointing a dead body (Mark 16:1); the disciples were convinced and believed He was dead and His resurrection was a great surprise to them (Matthew 28:17; Luke 24:37ff; John 20:3-9). Paul said that *"Christ died for our sins in accordance with the Scriptures, that he was buried, that he was raised on the third day in accordance with the Scriptures"* (1 Corinthians 15:2-4). If He did not die, then He would not have been buried. This is more evidence that Jesus did die.

Some who claim to believe in the resurrection of Christ refuse to believe that His was a bodily resurrection. They explain that at His resurrection He passed out of His physical life, into His spiritual life. However, the evidence would make it clear that the resurrection of Christ was a bodily resurrection.

Several things prove that Christ arose bodily. Jesus Himself said after His resurrection that He had flesh and bones (Luke 24:39). Matthew recorded that the women who met Christ on the resurrection morning *"took hold of his feet and worshipped him"* (Matthew 28:9). Christ ate some broiled fish in the presence of

His disciples after He had risen (Luke 24:40-43). Jesus invited His disciples to see and touch Him, as a ghost does not have flesh and bones (Luke 24:34-39). The signs of His crucifixion were also visible.

From the Scriptures we learn that the body of Jesus had undergone a remarkable change, and could suddenly appear and disappear in a surprising manner (Luke 24:31,36; John 20:13,19; 21:7). He was endowed with new qualities perfectly adjusted in His future heavenly environment. His disciples had gathered in a room with the doors locked when Jesus suddenly appeared to them. He appeared to the two disciples on the road to Emmaus, to Mary of Magdala, and to the disciples on the Sea of Galilee.

Christ's resurrected body was *real*, not a figment of imagination, not an aberration, not a ghost, but actually there, walking, talking, eating, appearing and vanishing among the disciples in exactly the way Christ intended. The resurrected body possessed characteristics which are not true of our bodies.

Christ's resurrection is the sign and pledge of the resurrection of the body for all who are in Christ, and determines the Christian's new attitude to death and transforms their hope for the future (1 Corinthians 15:12-58; Acts 4:2; 26:23; Romans 8:10-11; 2 Corinthians 4:14).

Jesus is the Resurrection and the Life

On one occasion Jesus was with His disciples when a message came to them that His friend Lazarus was sick. However, Jesus did not rush to Bethany, nor did He heal him from a distance as He did the Centurion's servant (Matthew 8:5,13), but remained where He was. Two days later He said to His disciples that they should go back to Judea for their friend Lazarus was sleeping and He was going to wake him up. The disciples thought that if Lazarus had fallen into a natural sleep he was getting better but Jesus was telling them that Lazarus was now dead. Death for the believer is compared to "sleep".

When Jesus and His disciples came near to Bethany they found that Lazarus had been in the grave for four days. Martha and Mary said to Jesus that if He had come earlier, Lazarus would not have died, showing the faith they had in their Master, but Jesus told Martha that her brother would rise again. Martha showed her faith in the resurrection when she said, *"I know that he will rise again in the resurrection at the last day"* (John 11:24). Martha was looking to the future, knowing that Lazarus would rise again in the last day when the resurrection takes place and she would see him.

Then Jesus said to her, *"I am the resurrection and the life. Whoever believes in me, though he die, yet shall he live, and everyone who lives and believes in me shall never die. Do you believe this?"* (John 11:25-26).

They took Jesus to the tomb of Lazarus and when they got there our Lord once again showed His compassion for His friends and we are told, *"Jesus wept"* (John 11:35). Why did Jesus weep, knowing that He would soon raise Lazarus from the dead (v.11)? It showed Jesus' humanity and seeing those around Him weeping at the loss of a family member He also shared in their grief, they were tears of genuine sympathy, showing it is never wrong to weep at the death of a loved one. Some of those present saw this and said, *"See how he loved him!"* (v.36) and others said *"Could not he who opened the eyes of the blind man also have kept this man from dying?"* (v.37). The suggestion has been made that they may have been tears of regret and if He had come sooner, He could have prevented this sadness in the family He loved.

Some commentators suggest that although Jesus knew Mary and Martha's tears would soon be turned to joy, He wept for Lazarus; knowing that He was about to call His friend back from heaven to a wicked sinful world, where he would one day have to die again. Jesus had come down from heaven and He knew what it was like and therefore what Lazarus would soon have to experience. Can anyone imagine what it would be like to be in heaven where there is no sin or sickness or death or sorrow and then to have to leave it?

When Jesus asked for the stone to be removed from the tomb, Martha protested saying, *"Lord, by this time there will be an odour, for he has been dead four days"* (v.39). Therefore we cannot doubt that Lazarus had actually died and they were about to witness a mighty miracle. With the stone rolled away Jesus offered up a prayer to His Father and then called out with a loud voice, *"Lazarus, come out"* (v.43). Many people have pointed out that if Jesus had not singled out Lazarus, He would have emptied the whole cemetery, but He shouted, *"Lazarus come out".*

Lazarus appeared at the entrance of the tomb with *"his hands and feet bound with linen strips, and his face wrapped with a cloth. Jesus said to them, "Unbind him, and let him go"* (v.44). Obviously, Lazarus would have been unable to walk with his feet bound, to the entrance of the tomb, so the Spirit of God must have carried him along. This was truly an amazing miracle.

Here we have an account of Lazarus being raised from the dead, how did his rising differ from that of Jesus? The answer lies in the fact that Jesus raised Lazarus from the dead and one day he would die again, but Jesus' resurrection was unique. He was raised by His own power and He did not die again, He ascended into heaven and lives today. That is why He could say, *"I am the resurrection and the Life"* and because of that we have the assurance that one day we too will rise from the dead.

In what body will we arise at the Resurrection?

Having considered the resurrection of our Lord Jesus Christ, Paul deals with another problem that has caused concern and some anxiety to many - when we experience the resurrection, in what body will we arise? (1 Corinthians 15:35-49).

We may be able to understand that if we should be living when Jesus returns, He would be able to change our bodies into immortality. However, if we should die before Christ returns and our bodies are laid to rest in the grave for hundreds or thousands of years then it is difficult to understand how it could be raised again.

Paul answers that concern when he says, *"someone will ask, "How are the dead raised? With what kind of body do they come?"* (1 Corinthians 15:35). He proceeds to answer that question by giving the illustration from nature. When the farmer sows his grain he knows that when it falls into the ground it will rot and die, but that is not the end of the seed. He knows that it will come to life again - first a blade of green, then several ears bearing many seeds like the one he planted.

The actual seed that was planted no longer exists, yet it has come to life again. The seed must be destroyed if the new life is to appear - new life does not come unless the grain first 'dies'. *"What you sow does not come to life unless it dies. And what you sow is not the body that is to be, but a bare seed, perhaps of wheat or of some other grain. But God gives it a body as he has chosen, and to each kind of seed its own body"* (1Corinthians 15:36-38).

In fact, it is scientifically true that our body mostly replaces itself every seven to fifteen years. Therefore with the change of most elements, we receive new bodies on a regular basis. We may not be conscious of this change. Nevertheless we have not the same body today that we had several years ago. There is an identity that we maintain all our lifetime, and yet there is not one cell of our bodies that was there some years ago. In the resurrection our bodies will bear our individual identities.

Therefore, our resurrection bodies will be of the same nature as our current bodies. The substance and essence of them will be the same. When you plant barley you don't get corn. When you plant an apple tree you don't get an orange tree. The tree or the plant is of the same essence and nature as the seed. (1 Corinthians 15:35-50).

Therefore, if there are differences here on earth, why should we wonder about the difference between bodies suitable to earth and bodies befitting to heaven? *"There are heavenly bodies and earthly bodies, but the glory of the heavenly is of one kind, and the glory of the earthly is of another"* (1 Corinthians 15:40). Our Lord Jesus came into this world and took an "earthly body" but after having made atonement for our sins on the cross, He came forth in the resurrection, in a "heavenly body", and in that body He ascended through the heavens into the very presence of God where He "lives to make intercession" for us. His "heavenly body" is the pattern of what ours shall be; we shall have bodies in the resurrection that are not subject to the laws that control us now.

There is a natural body and there is a spiritual body. A few hours after death corruption begins in our "earthly bodies"; but the new body will be incorruptible; it will be a glorified body. Just what that means may be seen from what the disciples saw on the Mount of Transfiguration when Jesus took Peter, James and John with Him to a mountain to pray. They saw the Lord Jesus meet and talk with Moses and Elijah who "appeared in glory". Moses, a man who had died many years earlier, yet he was present in his glorified body and Elijah, a man caught up to heaven without dying, was also present in his glorified body.

Contrasting our earthly bodies with the brilliance of our heavenly (resurrected) bodies, Paul says, *"What is sown is perishable; what is raised is imperishable. It is sown in dishonour; it is raised in glory. It is sown in weakness; it is raised in power. It is sown a natural body; it is raised a spiritual body. If there is a natural body, there is also a spiritual body...."* (1 Corinthians 15:42-47). Therefore, one day our resurrected bodies will be spiritual, imperishable and will rise in glory and power.

Through the first Adam, we received our natural bodies, suitable for earthly surroundings. However, they became perishable as a result of the 'Fall' in the Garden of Eden. Because of Adam's disobedience, mankind became mortal and condemned to death. From dust we came and to dust we will return (Genesis 3:19; Ecclesiastes 3:20). Our resurrected bodies, on the other hand, will be "raised imperishable." They will never experience sickness, decay, deterioration or death. And *"when the perishable puts on the imperishable, and the mortal puts on immortality, then shall come to pass the saying that is written: 'Death is swallowed up in victory'"* (1 Corinthians 15:54).

In St. Peter's church graveyard in the village of Tewin, England, one grave stands out from all the rest. Growing out of the grave is one of the largest trees in the country. It stands as a great four-trunked tree (four trees from one root) growing out of the grave. Its presence has given rise to much speculation. The grave, from which this enormous tree grows, is that of Lady Anne Grimston. It is reported that Lady Anne Grimston did not believe in life after death. She denied that she would be resurrected from the dead and that when she lay dying in her luxurious home, she remarked to a friend, "I shall live again as surely as a tree will grow from my body." Lady Anne died in 1757 and was buried in a marble tomb. The grave was then marked by a large marble slab and surrounded by an iron railing.

Years later, the marble slab was found to have moved a little and a small tree began to grow. The tree continued its growth, tilting the marble stone and breaking the marble until today, over two hundred years later; it has surrounded the tomb with its roots and has torn the railing out of the ground with its massive trunks. To the unbeliever, this may be viewed as a coincidence. However, to the believer, it could be viewed as God's extraordinary intervention.

Let us therefore have no doubt that whether we may, or may not believe in life after death it will come to pass one day for each and every one of us.

The Bible Teaches the Resurrection of the Saved and those not Saved

Christians are to view their own death with joy, knowing that after death they will be with Christ. This is what the apostle Paul said, "*We are of good courage, and we would rather be away from the body and at home with the Lord*" (2 Corinthians 5:8). "*I am hard pressed between the two. My desire is to depart and be with Christ, for that is far better*" (Philippians 1:23).

Jesus brought the resurrection to the fore in the most outstanding way, for He clearly and regularly confirmed it. He said, "*Do not marvel at this, for an hour is coming when all who are in the tombs will hear his voice and come out, those who have done good to the resurrection of life, and those who have done evil to the resurrection of judgement*" (John 5:28). When Paul was on trial before Felix and the Jews he said, "*I worship the God of our fathers, believing everything laid down by the Law and written in the Prophets, having a hope in God, which these men themselves accept, that there will be a resurrection of both the just and the unjust* (Acts 24:14-15).

The Bible teaches the resurrection of the unsaved as well as the resurrection of the saints. "*And many of those who sleep in the dust of the earth shall awake, some to everlasting life, and some to shame and everlasting contempt*" (Daniel 12:2). The unsaved will be resurrected to stand in the final judgment. Those who have rejected God's salvation will be judged accordingly: "*And I saw the dead, great and small, standing before the throne, and books were opened. Then another book was opened, which is the book of life. And the dead were judged by what was written in the books, according to what they had done. Then Death and Hades were thrown into the lake of fire. This is the second death, the lake of fire*" (Revelation 20:12-14).

After the resurrection there will be no second chance to make amends for those who have rejected Christ. Scripture reminds us that the Lord Jesus will come from heaven with His angels, "*in flaming fire, inflicting vengeance on those who do not know God and on those who do not obey the gospel of our Lord Jesus. They will suffer the punishment of eternal destruction, away from the presence of the Lord and from the glory of his might*" (2 Thessalonians 1:8-9).

There are those who deny the resurrection of the unsaved and the final judgment. Some prefer to believe in universal or near-universal salvation. Such people deny the reality of the utter sinfulness of man, and believe in a salvation by works. This, of course denies the clear teaching of Scripture; *"For by grace you have been saved through faith. And this is not your own doing; it is the gift of God, not a result of works, so that no one may boast"* (Ephesians 2:8-9). God cannot tolerate sin; any sin will be enough to bring condemnation and eternal separation from God's grace. Since the unrepentant sinner will have rejected Christ's offer of salvation, they will have to pay the price themselves.

Scripture never encourages us to think that people will have a second chance to trust in Christ after death. Both the parable of the rich man and Lazarus (Luke 16:24-26) and the statement about death and judgement in Hebrews, makes this clear, *"And just as it is appointed for man to die once, and after that comes judgement"* (Hebrews 9:27).

When a loved one dies who has trusted in Christ for salvation we are told, *"you may not grieve as others do who have no hope. For since we believe that Jesus died and rose again, even so, through Jesus, God will bring with him those who have fallen asleep....."* (1 Thessalonians 4:13-14). However, the sorrow felt at the death of someone, who we understand has not trusted in Christ for salvation, is not a sorrow mixed with hope. When the apostle Paul thought about fellow Jews who had rejected Christ he said, *"I have great sorrow and unceasing anguish in my heart"* (Romans 9:2).

Therefore, there is great urgency to make sure of the most serious and life changing decision of our lives that we have trusted in Christ for salvation. We must make that decision in this life for there is no opportunity to do it after death. The wonderful news is that God raised the Lord and WILL also raise the believer up by His power to be with Him forever (1 Corinthians 6:14). Jesus gives us this promise: *"This is the WILL of him who sent me, that I shall lose none of all that he has given, but raise them up at the last day"* (John 6:39).

Questions for Reflection

1. Are you convinced that Christ rose from the dead?

2. Why was it necessary for Christ to rise from the dead?

3. What was the nature of the body in which Christ rose?

4. Are you persuaded that one day you will rise from the dead?

5. Are you a Christian and looking forward to being with your Saviour for eternity?

9
Jesus said, "I Will" Come Again

"Let not your hearts be troubled. Believe in God; believe also in me. In my Father's house are many rooms. If it were not so, would I have told you that I go to prepare a place for you? And if I go and prepare a place for you, I WILL come again and will take you to myself, that where I am you may be also"
(John 14:1-3)

For centuries the prophets in the Old Testament pointed towards the first coming of Christ. When Jesus did come, the Jews did not recognise Him, because they thought that the Messiah would come as a King, but instead He came as a humble baby into a poor family.

After living on this earth for over thirty years, Jesus told His disciples in the Upper Room He was leaving them for a while but that He would be coming back.

Forty days after Jesus' death and resurrection, He left earth and returned to heaven where He came from. The Ascension of Jesus to heaven was witnessed by His disciples and as a cloud hid Him from their view two men in white appeared and said, *"Men of Galilee, why do you stand looking into heaven? This Jesus, who was taken up from you into heaven, WILL come in the same way as you saw him go into heaven"* (Acts 1:11). The Christian hope is the expectation of the future return of our Lord. This teaching is known as the

Second Coming of Christ. The Scriptures plainly teach us to expect a literal, bodily return of Jesus Christ.

Every word that Jesus said is true. He said He would die and rise again on the third day, and He did. He said that He was coming back some day, and He will. The Second Coming of Christ is the greatest certainty of the future.

Several terms are used in the New Testament to announce this great event.

a) *Parousia* (lit. Presence) is the commonest term used in the Greek NT for the second coming of Christ. (Matthew 24:3; 1 Corinthians 15:23; 1 Thessalonians 2:19; 2 Thessalonians 2:1,8; 2 Peter 1:16). It means 'coming', 'arrival' or 'presence' and was used in the first century for the visit of an emperor or other distinguished person. It conveys the idea that the Lord's return will be a definite and decisive action on His part. He will come as surely as He came as a baby to Bethlehem. It will be the return of the King (Luke 19:12).

b) *Apokalypsis* (unveiling) means 'revelation' which points to the removal of that which now obstructs our vision of Christ (1 Corinthians 1:7; 2 Thessalonians 1:7; 1 Peter 1:7). The Lord's coming will reveal who He is and it will be the time for things, which are now hidden, to come to light.

c) *Epiphaneia* means 'appearing' or 'manifestation', a term referring to Christ's coming forth out of a hidden background with the rich blessings of salvation (2 Thessalonians 2:8; Titus 2:13). It also carries the idea of drawing back a veil so that what is there may be truly seen for what it is. It is clear that He who came to Bethlehem as a baby will be returning – as personal, as definite, as positive, and as real in human history as was His first coming. Christ shall appear a second time – there is no escape from the simple meaning of these words. We wait for Christ's return to earth.

Jesus came the first time to a cattle shed in an obscure village with only a few witnesses. He came to deal with the problem of our sin and to bring salvation to mankind. Joseph was told to take Mary as his wife, *"for that which is conceived in her is from the Holy Spirit. She will bear a son, and you shall call his name Jesus, for he will save his people from their sin"* (Matthew 1:20-21). When He comes again, however, He will come in glory. The Bible says, *"Behold, he is coming with the clouds, and every eye will see him"* (Revelation 1:7). When He returns all mankind will know about it and shall see Him. Paul in all his writings is conscious of this truth of the Second Coming of Christ. He writes, *"the Lord Himself shall descend from heaven, with a shout... so shall we ever be with the Lord"* (1 Thessalonians 4:16-17).

Christ's second coming won't be hidden or secret—and the reason is because He will come to reign over all the earth as *"King of kings and Lord of lords"* (1 Timothy 6:15). History as we know it will come to an end, and a new day will dawn—a time of perfect righteousness and peace. The Bible says, *"When the Son of Man comes in his glory, and all the angels with him, then he will sit on his glorious throne"* (Matthew 25:31).

Why will Christ Return?

Jesus said, *"And if I go and prepare a place for you, I WILL come again and will take you to myself, that where I am you may be also"* (John 14:3). His return has special reference to His Church, to the Jews, to the world and to Satan. But here in John 14:1-3 He is speaking to His own followers, including those who today belong to Him.

What is the purpose of His return for His own people?

a) Jesus will come again to take His people home to heaven

Jesus has promised that He is coming back to gather to Himself all those who are His. *"I WILL come again and will take you to myself."* Paul said, Jesus will receive *"at his coming those who belong to Christ*" (1 Corinthians 15:23). The place Jesus is preparing has many rooms. Notice the significance of His words "*If it were not so, I would have told you*" (John 14:2). Jesus is coming back to take Christians to their heavenly home where they shall be freed from sin and earth's restrictions, to enjoy His presence for ever.

One day there will be a reunion with the Lord Himself, "*that where I am you may be also*" (John 14:3). When Jesus was praying to His Father for all believers, He said, "*Father, I desire that they also, whom you have given me, may be with me where I am, to see my glory*" (John 17:24). This then is why Christ has promised to return.

Jesus will never be satisfied until every one of His redeemed people is with Him in glory in the Father's house. Christians are not going to heaven because they deserve to go there, but are going because they have become a new creation (2 Corinthians 5:17), and children of God (John 1:12), through Christ Jesus. The Lord Jesus Christ is preparing a place for the Christian and the Father's house is for all the Father's children. Not everybody is going to heaven, but only those who have put their trust in Jesus Christ (Acts 4:12; 1 Timothy 2:4-6). The disciples were troubled because Jesus said He was going to leave them, but they must have been encouraged by the promise that He would return.

b) Jesus Christ will return to fulfil the promises of God

More than 100 prophecies dealing with Christ's birth, life and death were literally fulfilled.

A careful look at Old Testament prophecies shows an underlying assumption of two advents. Many Old Testament prophecies foretell the ultimate triumph of Christ, which will occur at the second coming. These include statements from the books of Zechariah 12:10-14; 9:14-15; Amos 9:11-15; Jeremiah 30:18; 32:44; 33:11; and Joel 3:1 which describe the Messiah coming in triumph to lead Israel into salvation. Also, Scripture records Jesus making direct comparisons to Old Testament prophecies when making His own claims to a second advent. For example, His words in Matthew 24:31 and Mark 13:27 parallel the descriptions of Isaiah 52:15 and Isaiah 59-62.

The Hebrew Scriptures indicate that the Promised One would appear, be cut off, and then reappear in victory. The first advent has occurred; the second is still future. The return of Jesus Christ is a vital part of God's redemptive plan for humanity. That's why the event was foretold by prophets, proclaimed by angels, and taught by Jesus and Paul. In fact, more Old Testament passages are devoted to Christ's Second Coming than to His first. In the New Testament, the Lord mentions His return more frequently than He speaks of His death.

c) Jesus Christ will return to keep His own promise

Christ's earthly teaching was filled with references to His Second Coming (Matthew 24-25; Luke 21). When He was on trial for His life, Jesus defended His own deity with a bold declaration of the Second Coming in the most triumphant terms. He told the High Priest, *"you will see the Son of Man seated at the right hand of Power, and coming with the clouds of heaven"* (Mark 14:62). On the night of His betrayal, Christ told the disciples, *"I go to prepare a place for you... I will come again and will take you to myself, that where I am you may be also"* (John 14:2-3). Not only is the credibility of God at stake in the Second Coming, but so is the credibility of His Son.

The Second Coming is when Jesus Christ will return to earth in fulfilment of His own promises. Jesus promised, *"then will appear in heaven the sign of the Son of Man, and then all the tribes of the earth will mourn, and they will see the Son of Man coming on the clouds of heaven with power and great glory"* (Matthew 24:30; Revelation 19:11-12).

Heaven is a place where Christ shall be present and where the Christian will be. He said, *"Where I am you may be also."* This is a *very comforting account of heaven for every Christian.* Heaven is our Father's house *and Jesus is there now, preparing a place for those who are His.* Are we ready to meet Him when He comes and fulfils His word *"I will come back?"* Will He receive us to Himself because we belong to Him, or will He have to reject us (Matthew 25:10-13)?

How will Christ return?

When the disciples stood looking up as Jesus ascended into heaven, there appeared two angels who said to them, *"Men of Galilee, why do you stand looking into heaven? This Jesus, who was taken up from you into heaven, WILL come in the same way as you saw him go into heaven"* (Acts 1:11). Jesus ascended bodily into heaven, and He will return bodily. He took His flesh and bones with Him. After His resurrection He said to His disciples, *"See my hands and my feet, that it is I myself. Touch me, and see. For a spirit does not have flesh and bones as you see that I have"* (Luke 24:39).

a) It will be a physical coming

Jesus will return to earth in the body, it will be a literal, physical return of Jesus from heaven to earth. It will be a visible coming. It will be a *'glorious coming'* in *'power and great glory'* (Matthew 20:30) *'every eye will see him'* (Revelation 1:7; Acts 1:11; Hebrews 9:28). Christ ascended into heaven from where He will come again. The Nicene Creed (AD 325) uses very similar language, and the Athanasian Creed is slightly more explicit:

"He ascended into heaven, He sits at the right hand of the Father, God Almighty, from whence He will come to judge the quick and the dead. At His coming all men will rise again with their bodies."

None of these extra-biblical documents, of course, are infallible, but they show that the Christians of the earliest centuries clearly understood the plain biblical promises to point to a literal, future, bodily return of Jesus. We see this hope of Jesus' return from heaven to earth repeated again in the Apostles' preaching.

"Repent therefore, and turn back, that your sins may be blotted out, that times of refreshing may come from the presence of the Lord, and that he may send the Christ appointed for you, Jesus, whom heaven must receive until the time for restoring all the things about which God spoke by the mouth of his holy prophets long ago" (Acts 3:19-21).

The resurrected body of Christ had certain characteristics - the body was real, visible, capable of being handled and recognisable. Yet at the same time it was able to pass through solid objects and disappear.

b) It will be a glorious and triumphant coming

Though personal, physical and visible it will be very different from His first coming. He will not return in the body of His humiliation, but in a glorified body and in royal apparel. *"So Christ, having been offered once to bear the sins of many, will appear a second time, not to deal with sin but to save those who are eagerly waiting for him"* (Hebrews 9:28).

Paul said, *"For the Lord himself will descend from heaven with a cry of command, with the voice of an archangel, and with the sound of the trumpet of God. And the dead in Christ will rise first. Then we who are alive, who are left, will be caught up together with them in the clouds to meet the Lord in the air, and so we will always be with the Lord. Therefore encourage one another with these words"* (1 Thessalonians 4:13-18).

The Second Coming will be in contrast to the Firs

The writer to the Hebrews explains not only the fact of the Second Advent but also the meaning of it. Jesus came in the first

Advent to reveal what sin was and deal with it and He will come again to set up His Kingdom (Hebrews 9:28).

Therefore having finally dealt with sin on the cross in His first Advent, Jesus' next coming, His Second Advent, is to be that of victory. At the first Advent He was born in a cattle shed where only a few people knew about it, when He comes again everyone will know about it. The Second Coming of Christ will be *"with power and great glory."* Perhaps the best way to understand that statement is to compare the circumstances surrounding the first and second comings.

The first time Jesus came unnoticed into the world, the second time *"every eye will see him."* In his first coming Jesus humbled himself, being born in a stable in Bethlehem. When He returns, He will come back as King of Kings and Lord of Lords. In His first coming He endured the mockery of men who despised Him for his goodness. Although He was the Son of God, He allowed them to put Him to death, that He might provide salvation for the world. When He comes again He will rule the nations with a rod of iron. He came the first time as the Lamb of God; He will come again as the Lion of the Tribe of Judah.

Two thousand years ago the religious leaders shouted in scorn, *"He saved others, but he can't save himself!"* (Matthew 24:42). The day is coming when the whole world will see Jesus as He really is. When that happens, every knee will bow and every tongue will confess that Jesus Christ is Lord, to the glory of God the Father (Philippians 2:9-11).

There will be no doubt on the minds of anyone on this planet as to what has happened when the King of kings re-appears. When Jesus returns it will be in triumph for ALL to see.

One day prophecy will be fulfilled. Christ WILL return to earth and everyone will see and know that this great event has taken place.

When will Christ return?

In Mark 13:32 we read, *"But concerning that day or that hour, no one knows, not even the angels in heaven, nor the Son, but only the Father."*

a) Christ's return is known only to the Father

The world waited for 4,000 years, and then Jesus came as a baby to Bethlehem. He was here only 33 years and then He left after His crucifixion and resurrection. But He left a promise that He would come again. As the world watched and waited for His first coming, and He came, so now we watch and wait for His appearing, a second time.

This verse has been the focus of much debate. Some have used it to demonstrate that Jesus could not be truly God because God is all-knowing and Jesus here admits there is something His Father knows that He does not. The question has often been asked, 'how can the Lord Jesus be ignorant of anything, since He is God and says Himself, *"I and the Father are one"* (John 10:30) and again He said, *"Have I been with you so long, and you still do not know me, Philip? Whoever has seen me has seen the Father. How can you say, 'Show us the Father'* (John 14:9)? Why then would Jesus say He did not know when He would return if He truly was equal with His Father?

What does it mean that the Son does not know? Has Mark now put in danger, or is he denying, the divinity of Christ? Has the text been corrupted, or is there another meaning for "know"? So remarkable is Mark's statement about Christ's ignorance that Ralph P. Martin concluded that the verse "has been an exegetical embarrassment from the beginning."

However, we must recognise that when Jesus was on earth He was both God and man (John 1:1, 14; 20:28; Colossians 2:9), and during His ministry in Jerusalem, He was co-operating with the limitations of being a man. As a man, Jesus walked and talked. There is the deep mystery of the union of two natures where both are found together in His Person. We also know it is impossible for mortal man to explain this. We can only say, in the present instance, that our Lord spoke as a man, and not as God.

The vast majority of evangelical theologians today hold a two-nature solution to Mark 13:32. This solution is the result of many years of debate, where the nature of Christ and the nature of His incarnation were debated. The two-nature approach owes its present form to the council of Chalcedon in AD 451. The Chalcedonian creed was a landmark in church history, and continues to hold a central part in modern Christology. The Chalcedonian Definition, stating that Jesus is "perfect both in deity and in humanness; this selfsame one is also actually God and actually man."

The Christian theologian and Church Father Athanasius (c.296-373), the chief defender of the full deity of the Lord Jesus Christ against the nontrinitarian teaching of 4th century (Trinitarianism against Arianism), led the way in the final solution. He proposed that a two-nature model would answer the problem of Mark 13:32. Athanasius's answer to the problem of the ignorance of the Son is that when Jesus said that the Son did not know, He spoke according to His humanity, not His divinity. "Son" refers to the humanity of Christ in this passage, not to the deity. Since then many have accepted and built upon the two-nature structure. Hence, both the humanity and the divinity of Christ are upheld without bringing either into jeopardy; and the two-nature solution is not limited to Mark 13:32; it can be used to explain how Jesus was tempted as man, but He conquered as God; He hungered as man but as God could feed thousands; He was weary as man but as God He could give rest.

The apostle Paul explains how Jesus *"made Himself of no reputation, and took upon him the form of a servant, and was made in the likeness of men"* (Philippians 2:7). While we cannot explain all aspects of Christ making *"Himself of no reputation"* and was made *"in the likeness of men"* it seems clear that Christ intentionally and temporarily laid aside certain elements of His power when He took on human form. We can see this throughout the Gospels as Christ was constantly depending upon His Father, and yet was doing everything the Father did, and in the same manner (e.g. John 5:19ff & 30).

b) The return of Jesus Christ is likened to the coming of a thief in the night

Two passages use the wording, 'a thief in the night'. *"But know this, that if the master of the house had known in what part of the night the thief was coming, he would have stayed awake and would not have let his house be broken into"* (Matthew 24:43): *"For you yourselves are fully aware that the day of the Lord will come like a thief in the night"* (1 Thessalonians 5:2).

Just as a thief catches a household by surprise under the cover of darkness, Jesus will catch the unbelieving world by surprise when He returns in judgment. People will be *"eating and drinking, marrying and giving in marriage"* (verse 38), just as if they have all the time in the world. But then, before they know it, Judgment Day will be upon them (verses 40–41). Paul puts it this way: *"While people are saying, 'There is peace and security,' then sudden destruction will come upon them as labour pains come upon a pregnant woman, and they will not escape"* (1 Thessalonians 5:3).

The apostle Paul said, *"Now concerning the times and the seasons, brothers, you have no need to have anything written to you"* (1 Thessalonians 5:1). Paul had just noted that his readers did not need information about the exact time or season Jesus would return. Instead, Jesus would return at any moment, unexpectedly like a thief in the night.

c) The return of Jesus Christ is likened to the days of Noah

What will be the signs of Jesus' coming and the end of the world? This was the very same question Jesus' disciples asked. Jesus' answer to them and to us is found in Matthew 24:37-39: *"For as were the days of Noah, so will be the coming of the Son of Man. For as in those days before the flood they were eating and drinking, marrying and giving in marriage, until the day when Noah entered the ark, and they were unaware until the flood came and swept them all away, so will be the coming of the Son of Man."*

There was no awareness that the judgment of God was about to fall upon them in Noah's day. They did not realize anything was wrong until Noah went into the ark and the rain began to fall. We look at the deteriorating moral values in our nation – the divorce rate, abortion, pornography, drug addiction, child abuse and see what has transpired in the homosexual community. We are shocked at the violent crimes, the drive-by shootings and the terrorism that plagues our world. People do not realize how the wickedness of the world today is very much like it was in the days of Noah. Jesus pointed out that in Noah's day the people were totally oblivious to the coming judgement of God.

In His major end-time prophecy, Jesus answers the question posed by the disciples: *"Tell us, when will these things be, and what will be the sign of your coming and of the end of the age?"* (Matthew 24:3). After listing a number of signs of the nearness of His coming, He reveals that *"this gospel of the kingdom will be proclaimed throughout the whole world as a testimony to all nations, and then the end will come"* (Matthew 24:14).

This generation has seen global communication through television, Internet, social media and telephone in such a way never experienced before and it is possible to reach around the world with the Gospel of Jesus Christ. Almost anyone in the world with access to the Internet could watch and hear a gospel presentation.

It is possible that within a few years every tribe and nation will have access to the truth of Jesus Christ.

Apparently, there is going to be much deception about Jesus' Second Coming. But God will not allow even Satan to fully copy how Jesus is to come. We know this is true because Jesus specifically warns us how He is to return. All others are imposters! If people say they are one of the dead prophets or even Christ or if even Satan comes as Christ! We are told not to believe any of these reports or even what we see because Christ's coming will be a very public event! For as lightning comes from the east to the west, covering the entire sky; this is what it is going to be like when Jesus returns. If someone says Jesus has already come, you will know that it is not true! When Jesus returns, everyone will see it over the whole earth.

When Jesus returns at the end of the world to collect His Saints, He will gather them from all parts of the earth. Here we have three parallel accounts of what Jesus told His disciples about His second coming: Matthew 24:29-31; Mark 13:24-27; Luke 21:25-28 and so they are placed side by side and complement each other.

There is much debate and diversities of interpretation as to how and when Jesus will return. There are those who stress certain events must precede His return. Christians differ greatly in their interpretation however, we are told to look for His coming again. We are to pray for His return and ought to be comforted by it. Jesus did say, "I WILL come again."

Questions for Reflection

1. Why is it necessary for Christ to return one day?

2. What will Christ's return be like?

3. Do you think Christ's return is near? Give your reasons for and against.

4. How would you compare Christ's coming as a baby and His return?

5. What makes you think Christ will keep His promise, "I will come again"?

BV - #0033 - 040221 - C0 - 215/143/8 - PB - 9781620209820 - Gloss Lamination